SEEING BEYOND OUR LINE OF SIGHT

Consciously Moving
Through Life's
Changes, Transitions, and Deaths

Dr. Angela Brownemiller

**CONSCIOUSLY MOVING THROUGH
LIFE'S CHANGES, TRANSITIONS, AND DEATHS**

SEEING BEYOND OUR LINE OF SIGHT

SEEING BEYOND OUR LINE OF SIGHT

Consciously Moving

Through Life's

Changes, Transitions, and Deaths

Dr. Angela Brownemiller

KEYS TO
CONSCIOUSNESS AND SURVIVAL SERIES
Volume 10

Metaterra® Publications

**CONSCIOUSLY MOVING THROUGH
LIFE'S CHANGES, TRANSITIONS, AND DEATHS**

Metaterra® Publications
SEEING BEYOND OUR LINE OF SIGHT
Consciously Moving Through
Life's Changes, Transitions, and Deaths
KEYS TO CONSCIOUSNESS AND SURVIVAL SERIES, Volume 10
Copyright © 2021, 2020, 2019, 2015, 2010, 2005, 2000, 1998.
Angela Brownemiller / Angela Browne-Miller.
Copyright © 2021, 2020, 2000, Metaterra® Publications.
All rights reserved in all formats and in
all languages and dialects known or not known at this time.
Published in the United States by Metaterra® Publications.
HYPERLINK "http://www.Metaterra.com"
www.Metaterra.com   www.Amazon.com
Brownemiller, Angela.
SEEING BEYOND OUR LINE OF SIGHT:
CONSCIOUSLY MOVING THROUGH
LIFE'S CHANGES, TRANSITIONS, AND DEATHS
Metaterra/Angela Brownemiller/
1. Spiritual. 2. Metaphysical/Esoteric. 3. Consciousness. 4. Psychology.
5. Biology. 6. Well-Being. 7. Mental Health. 8. Addiction. 9. Depression.
10. Recovery. 11. Death and Dying. 12. Science.
13. Angela Brownemiller. 14. Angela Browne-Miller.
ISBN-13: ISBN 978-1-937951-49-8 (**Paperback**)
See also Amazon and website below for **Ebook** and **Audiobook**.
Published in the United States of America for US and worldwide distribution.
Metaterra® Publications, Metaterra.com
Seeing Beyond Our Line of Sight by and copyright © Angela Brownemiller.
Cover and book content, text, wording, titles, illustrations, charts, diagrams,
all interior and exterior content.
by and copyright ©Angela Brownemiller.
Book and cover design by and copyright ©Angela Brownemiller.
Ordering information and bulk ordering information available through:
Amazon Paperback, Amazon Kindle, Amazon Audible, iTunes, etc.
Metaterra.com   DrAngela.com
All rights to all copies, printings, forms, formats, editions, adaptations, and excerpts reserved. Without prior written and signed permission from the publisher, copyright holder, author, and illustrator, no part of this book (words, text, illustrations, diagrams, charts, or other) may be published, and or reproduced, copied, transcribed, distributed, transmitted, broadcast, and or stored, in any form and or by any means, (handwritten, typed, printed, spoken, taped, digital, virtual, audio, video, movie, and or other past, present, and or future digital, electronic, virtual, or other formats/forms, and or mechanical formats/forms, and or manual or vocal means). The exception to this rights restriction is only for the inclusion of a brief (20 to 30 word) quotation (credited to this book, author, illustrator, and publisher) in a professional review. Thank you.

SEEING BEYOND OUR LINE OF SIGHT

Dedicated to my ascended father,

Lee.

**CONSCIOUSLY MOVING THROUGH
LIFE'S CHANGES, TRANSITIONS, AND DEATHS**

SEEING BEYOND OUR LINE OF SIGHT

Life Light
Thread of life
weaves through time
liquid space
sand of being
dress of existing
pacing ourselves.
Dimensions we
cannot see
yet inhabit
know who we are
in increments.
Infinitesimal infinities
shrouding sensations
sensory limits
not heeded
realities
no longer needed.
Perception unfolds
myriad nows
beyond already here.
Time itself
a life form
cradling us
unpacks now
into beyond.
Legends who we are
mirrors of our minds
parallel universes
found selves waiting
for a name there
on the side of the road
street sign life
destination
light.

CONSCIOUSLY MOVING THROUGH
LIFE'S CHANGES, TRANSITIONS, AND DEATHS

SEEING BEYOND OUR LINE OF SIGHT

NOTE:

At first glance, a few of the chapters in this book (which is Volume 10 in this series) may somewhat resemble portions of Volume 2 in this KEYS TO CONSCIOUSNESS AND SURVIVAL SERIES, titled, ADVENTURES IN CHANGES, TRANSITIONS, AND DEATHS: PRIMER FOR LIFE'S MINOR AND MAJOR CHALLENGES AND PASSAGES.

However, do note that Volume 2 is in itself a PRIMER, setting out the basics of the material that all the books in this series build upon.

On other hand, this present book, Volume 10, is <u>reaching BEYOND the basics</u> to introduce the notion that we can not only already <u>SEE</u> OUR LINE OF SIGHT (as in Volume 2), we can also develop our own kingdom there to SEE and reach and even expand to realms **BEYOND** OUR LINE OF SIGHT (as in this volume, Volume 10). This expansion is imaginary or metaphorical perhaps, yet also psychological, for many also spiritual, and for some, can be perhaps developed by the mind or consciousness itself to become actual.

SEEING BEYOND OUR LINE OF SIGHT

Table of Contents

Dedication	5
Life Light	7
NOTE	15
Introduction	17
KEYS TO CONSCIOUSNESS AND SURVIVAL Series Foreword	19
*** To Readers	23
1. Introduction To Seeing Beyond Our Line Of Sight	25
PART ONE: Transition Awareness, Transition Management	37
2. Know Life's Transitional Nature	39
3. You CAN Ever More Consciously Navigate Transition	51
*** **Sensitizing To Landmarks Along The Path Of Transition** EXERCISE: General Transition Awareness	67
4. Consciously Entering Into Transition: The Idea Of Transition Management	75
5. Moving Beyond Limits We Are Told Exist	95
*** **IMPORTANT NOTE**	99
PART TWO: Fear Awareness-Es In Transition Processes	101
6. Overcoming The Apocalypse Syndrome	103
7. Personal Apocalypse	119

**CONSCIOUSLY MOVING THROUGH
LIFE'S CHANGES, TRANSITIONS, AND DEATHS**

PART THREE: Physical Death As Transition   125
8. Looking To The Frontier:
       Seeing And Extending Beyond Physical Death 127
9. Steps And Phases Of Death Transition   139
10. A First Phase Of Death   143
11. Cross Over Sensation   151
12. A Second Phase Of Death   163
*** **Basic Emotional Body Mapping EXERCISE**   175
13. A Third Phase Of Death   177
*** **CONTINUE TO EXIST NOTES**   178
*** **Basic Mental Body Mapping EXERCISE**   189

PART FOUR: Continuum Of Consciousness   191
14. Indistinct Boundaries Between Life And Death
       Shift To The Continuum   193
15. Introduction To The
       Continuum Of Consciousness   199
16. The Maze Of Consciousnesses (Diagram)   201
17. Overlapping Levels Of
       Perceived Consciousness (Diagram)   203
18. The Many Deaths (Diagram)   205
19. We Need Not Die (Diagram)   209
20. Transcending Physicality
       And Its Patterns (Diagram)   211

PART FIVE: Mastering Transition Along
       The Continuum Of Consciousness   213
21. Master Transition From
       One Reality To Another   215
22. Imagination For Exploration Of
       Transition Situations   223
23. Shifting The Self Through Transition   241

SEEING BEYOND OUR LINE OF SIGHT

24. Shed The Skin In Moving Through	247
25. How To Know Your Skin's Too Tight	253
26. Harvest Transition	263
*** PREPARE FOR THE HARVEST	**267**
27. Cosmic Democracy	271
PART SIX: Revolution	273
28. Ride Personal Expansion Into Personal and Species Power	275
29. Embrace The Revolution Brought By Conscious Death	283
30. The Right To Know The Art And Science Of Conscious Dying	289
31. Sense The Momentum	291
Epilog	293
Never Ending Stream	295
Appendices	297
Booklist And Recommended Reading	299
See These Books By Dr. Angela Brownemiller:	299-310
Seeing The Hidden Face Of Addiction	
Navigating Life's Stuff	
How To Die And Survive	
Unveiling The Hidden Instinct	
Ask Dr. Angela Series	
About The Author	**312**

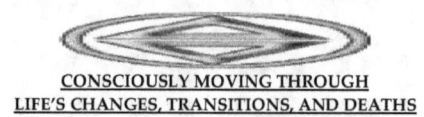
**CONSCIOUSLY MOVING THROUGH
LIFE'S CHANGES, TRANSITIONS, AND DEATHS**

SEEING BEYOND OUR LINE OF SIGHT

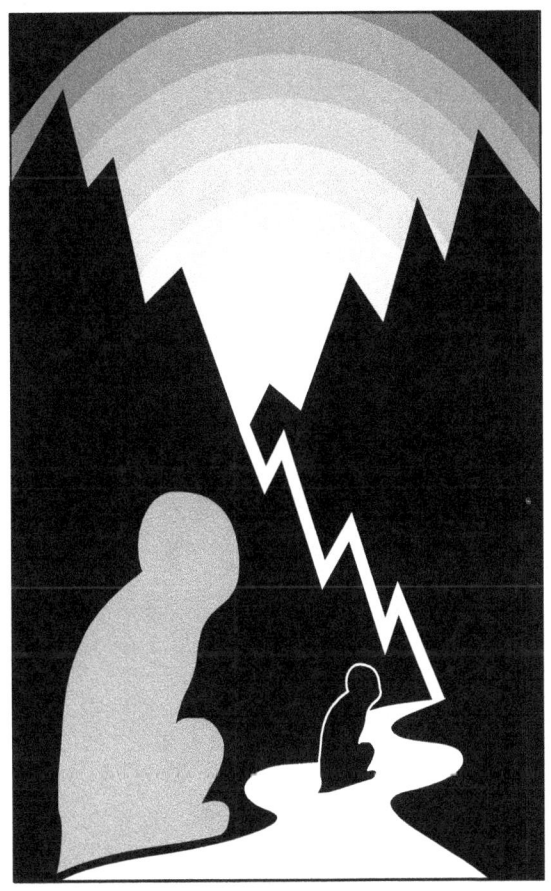

... though I walk
through the valley
of the shadow of death,
I will fear no evil ...
Psalm 23

**CONSCIOUSLY MOVING THROUGH
LIFE'S CHANGES, TRANSITIONS, AND DEATHS**

Introduction

One day, while walking along lost in deep thought, I found I had wandered a few steps ahead of myself, beyond my body. Startled, I turned around to see myself there, walking toward me. I stopped and waited a moment for my physical self to catch up, to merge with me, then walk as one with me.

A few steps later, I realized this moving ahead had happened again. This time, I allowed myself to continue moving ahead of myself, allowed my physical body to follow me. Being out of my body like this was a fascinating experience. Yet, I found I wanted not to lose my physical body, that it was my place for now. I felt more than certain I wanted to continue to travel in this physical vehicle, this biological body, through this physical plane world.

I knew one day I would move on, move beyond that physical vehicle to travel elsewhere in other ways. For now, I would simply live here and grow familiar with my journey beyond, with what is out there BEYOND my physical body's, my biological eyes', my current mind's, LINE OF SIGHT.

Where we live is where we believe we live. And, where we do actually live is indeed far BEYOND OUR LINE OF SIGHT. Perhaps accepting this, knowing this, preparing for this understanding, will ease the passages and transitions we find ourselves moving through every day, every minute, every moment, always.

The Author

**CONSCIOUSLY MOVING THROUGH
LIFE'S CHANGES, TRANSITIONS, AND DEATHS**

SEEING BEYOND OUR LINE OF SIGHT

KEYS TO CONSCIOUSNESS AND SURVIVAL
Series Foreword

Just as the fish itself did not discover water, we ourselves have perhaps inadvertently demonstrated the obvious, which is that we cannot entirely, absolutely, know what all it is "we" are immersed in, nor even what all it is that "we" are.

Ultimately, the question of the hour, the question of our times, the question of our reality, is regarding this "thing" we call our ever present "consciousness." How do we identify with our consciousness, is it of us, is it us, is it more than we are, or is it simply a side effect of life? While this term, **consciousness**, appears in a multitude of contexts, is even part of the popular jargon, what consciousness is and means remains unsettled, unproven, disputed. The full nature of consciousness itself is, even after centuries of Human discussion, still eluding us.

I suggest that the true question here is whether the amorphous consciousness is itself *derivative of biology*, or is itself

independent of biology (and perhaps even independent of what any intelligence can entirely discover of itself from within itself and its tools). I add, however, that even this question will reveal itself to be irrelevant.

This stunning shift in understanding will happen once we recognize that our seemingly elusive consciousness can at any point be redefined, or step forward and **redefine itself to itself and thus to us**—or even shift into (or back into) independence of biology, stepping out of evolutionary, synaptic, and conceptual controls. Once consciousness steps forward, moves into its existence <u>independent</u> of Human science, religion, philosophy, **even of the Human brain itself**—consciousness may (perhaps once again) elect to leave our physical bodies, much like a grown child leaving home.

As they depart, we can speculate that our consciousness-es are in a sense like our children, in that they apparently stem from us—a speculation no machine intelligence (as yet incapable of actual procreation and actual biological parental ties) will ever do unless consciously programmed to be able to do. Our children, once they consciously leave home, their consciousness-es in tow,

SEEING BEYOND OUR LINE OF SIGHT

can grow up to consciously be who they already are.

Get ready, even the Human Consciousness is going to break free of the **conceptual** confines of its biological host bodies here on Earth. It's been a nice visit but the time may come to go, or at least to **expand our awareness**.

Dr. Angela Brownemiller

NOTE: The following book frequently describes the plural of both the terms, *consciousness* and *awareness*, as *consciousness*-**es** and *awareness*-**es**, to further emphasize the dual individual and collective nature of both the *consciousness* and the *awareness*.

**CONSCIOUSLY MOVING THROUGH
LIFE'S CHANGES, TRANSITIONS, AND DEATHS**

SEEING BEYOND OUR LINE OF SIGHT

***

To Readers

This is a book of ideas, an exploration. Readers will note that this book is of course material presented to Readers, also to my workshop group participants and individual clients as they work through their own life issues and transition processes.

Although I do engage in diagnosis and treatment in my clinical work, I do not do this on the pages of this book. Please therefore note that the following is not itself diagnosis or treatment. Readers experiencing physical health or mental health conditions are urged to see a professional for diagnosis and treatment, ideally in person, or online where in person options are not available.

Dr. Angela Brownemiller
DrAngela.com

**CONSCIOUSLY MOVING THROUGH
LIFE'S CHANGES, TRANSITIONS, AND DEATHS**

1
Introduction To
Seeing Beyond Our Line Of Sight

The LINE OF SIGHT is generally viewed as an imaginary line. You know your LINE OF SIGHT. This line is said to extend from your eye to the object you are seeing. Some might describe this as the shortest distance between two points. Others will know that this LINE OF SIGHT may not be the shortest distance. Distance itself is subjective, is bendable, folding, expanding, collapsing, is always changing.

Meet Our Line Of Sight

A dear old friend long ago taught me to hold the LINE OF SIGHT in sailing, to stay aware of the goal, the destination point. This way, the sails, which would be adjusted along the way, would be adjusted to have the boat always continue toward the point, the destination. Reaching this destination would frequently involve zig zagging back and forth along or around the LINE OF SIGHT. Thus, the shortest distance between the two points, between the starting point and the destination point,

could be much longer than the distance directly along the given LINE OF SIGHT.

Unclear Lines

In life, our lines of sight are not always clear to us. We may not know exactly where we are going. We may be unsure of our ultimate destination. Or, our goals, our destinations, may change over time, or even change in an instant under sudden realization or sudden pressure.

In my work with persons experiencing life challenges, I have seen so many who say that they have lost their way, that they don't know where they are going, and that they don't even know why they are going where they are going.

I think back to the sailing metaphor. While the boat would not necessarily proceed directly along the LINE OF SIGHT, the tacks and turns would be taken back and forth around this line. The *process* of getting there, where ever this *there* might be, would be a journey in itself. And this journey would be essential. Indeed, this journey itself becomes the destination. In other words, the process, the transition, *is* the destination, the ongoing destination.

SEEING BEYOND OUR LINE OF SIGHT

This Is Our Journey

This is our journey. We are moving along, even zig zagging along, moving toward something that is not always clear to us.

Several of my clients have said, "Well, all there is is this: you get born, then you live, then you die. That's all." These absolute terms are, on the one hand, offering clarity, definition. And, on the other hand, these absolute terms are setting limits. These limits may be closing us out of, may not be suggesting, the full picture—or at least *the full range of possibilities.*

What if it is up to us whether this "that's all" is really accurate in saying that "that is all"? What if we can have a say, even increasing say, in whether that *really is* all, even in what all that *all* is.

See Beyond Limits

My view is that we Humans can consciously develop, evolve, ourselves to reach beyond the limits included in this "that is all." Where there may be a limit set for us now, it is up to us to reach beyond this limit, to SEE BEYOND OUR present LINE OF SIGHT. We can become ever more aware of the

awareness-es and capabilities we carry within ourselves, awareness-es and capabilities to see beyond these limits. (See other books in this KEYS TO CONSCIOUSNESS AND SURVIVAL SERIES for details on further developing this awareness.[1])

The "that is all there is" is not *all* there is. The destination expands beyond the end point, disappears from a set ending to a continuum. This is a *continuum of transition*.

I have long lived with the sense that holding one's LINE OF SIGHT in life is a powerful driver, a way of staying in touch with the meaning of one's life.

I have also come to sense that the so-called end point, the destination point, the goal of the LINE OF SIGHT, can be consciously extended once we are consciously aware that we have or can develop this option.

---

[1] See, for example, the book, UNVEILING THE HIDDEN INSTINCT: UNDERSTANDING OUR INTERDIMENSIONAL SURVIVAL AWARENESS, which is Volume 3 in this KEYS TO CONSCIOUSNESS AND SURVIVAL SERIES.

Reaching Beyond The Given Horizon

Over the years, I have worked with many persons experiencing life challenges, their own and or others' minor and major transitions, including but not limited to in-life as well as seeming end-of-life changes, transitions, and physical death and dying processes.

I have found that the perceived LINE OF SIGHT must reach past the given horizon, that the LINE OF SIGHT can be a point well beyond a physical ending, a physical death. Our LINE OF SIGHT can be continuous, ongoing rather than finite.

Our understanding of who we are is always evolving. We as individuals, and as a species, continue to seek increasing awareness of ourselves. We may not always see ourselves in this process; however, we are either subconsciously or consciously, or both, asking questions about the edges, the limits, we face.

My view is that our survival involves extending limits we have been told or led to believe we face. While these limits may in some ways be actual, these are *conceptual limits* themselves that we can *move our minds beyond*. We can consciously choose to SEE BEYOND OUR LINE OF SIGHT.

Defining Ourselves Beyond

When presented with death, actual physical, biological, death, questions regarding our defined limits, our limits on our limits themselves, can for many become front and center. We may ask these questions in simplified yet profound ways: What is happening when we die? Do I have any say in the death process? Is it possible that I can live on? What is death itself?

> **Ultimately, we are asking whether we can see anything beyond our given LINE OF SIGHT.**

There are also additional questions regarding death, questions this book suggests we must allow ourselves to ask: Do we know the full truth about death? Can death be *or become more* than what we have come to believe it is? Is my own belief regarding death working for me? Or, might I be able to add to this belief in ways that can help me *process this process* we call dying?

We can learn a great deal about the death transition by looking closely at in-life transition processes and experiences, their seen and unseen characteristics. Every minor and major

SEEING BEYOND OUR LINE OF SIGHT

transition process offers us the opportunity to SEE BEYOND OUR LINE OF SIGHT.

Recognize Windows

I tell my clients that general in-life issues, including the easier and the more challenging aspects of life, present us with opportunities to think a little or a lot outside the box. I add that, actually, life may not only present us with such opportunities, but life may also take us to the space *already outside the conceptual, philosophical, intellectual, whatever box we (think we) have been living in.*

If we are looking closely, our lives are constantly presenting us with openings to move outside our own boxes. Look around, see that we are already living outside our own boxes. We can indeed see this, and apply this to our understanding of what and who we are, and of what we are experiencing.

We can *sensitize ourselves* to hitherto unseen or only partially recognized *windows of opportunity*. These windows are actually *openings in awareness*. These windows of opportunity appear all around us, if we are watching for them.

CONSCIOUSLY MOVING THROUGH
LIFE'S CHANGES, TRANSITIONS, AND DEATHS

It is up to us to ever more consciously recognize these and then ever more consciously move ourselves into and through them.[2]

This Book Introduces

This book introduces my work in this area, sharing ideas that I delve into more deeply in other books in this KEYS TO CONSCIOUSNESS AND SURVIVAL SERIES. Herein, the goal of this book is to cover a lot of territory as quickly as possible. In so doing, I introduce several KEY concepts that I explain on the following pages, and then further develop in other books.

Here are a few of these concepts:

- Primary in this discussion is the notion of what this book defines as *conscious transition management*, asking, how can we bring to ourselves an *ever more conscious awareness and navigation of our transitions?*

---

[2] I share some concepts for *moving through* what I define as being *windows of opportunity* and *openings in awareness*, in the NAVIGATING LIFE'S STUFF books, Volumes 8 and 9 in this KEYS TO CONSCIOUSNESS AND SURVIVAL SERIES. See reading list at the end of this present book.

SEEING BEYOND OUR LINE OF SIGHT

- The KEY understanding here is that *all changes are transitions*, and that everything is always in transition.

- Also KEY here, is the realization that *all transitions move us through changes, such as amendments of, shifts in, endings of, in essence deaths of, some parts or pieces of our passages and their patterns.*

- In this sense, life brings us minor and major endings, deaths, almost every day we live.

- We are generally unaware that we are always moving through these endings, these in-life as well as seeming end-of-life deaths, that *we are always in the process of minor and major transition.*

- Life is always training us for **navigating and surviving transitions**, for **surviving changes and endings**, even **what may feel to be deaths**, for **navigating our transformations** of ourselves as we move through life's passages and their patterns.

**CONSCIOUSLY MOVING THROUGH
LIFE'S CHANGES, TRANSITIONS, AND DEATHS**

- Central in the material on the following pages is the notion that we each have, and actually are, our own *pattern* *of being*.

- Understanding this about ourselves is KEY in our *consciously moving through* minor and major in-life transitions, as well as seeming end-of-life transitions such as physical body death.

- We are, in essence, **patterns of being** moving through other patterns.

- However, we are not the environment, not the patterns we are moving *through*. We can become ever more aware of this distinction between ourselves, our own pattern of being, and the patterns we are moving through.

- Being ever more conscious of our own personal *pattern of being* can allow us to hold onto ourselves, our awareness, our consciousness, through our in-life as well as seeming end-of-life transitions.[3]

---

[3] This matter is detailed in the NAVIGATING LIFE'S STUFF books which are Volumes 8 and 9 in this KEYS TO CONSCIOUSNESS AND SURVIVAL SERIES.

SEEING BEYOND OUR LINE OF SIGHT

- We can become ever more sensitized to the nature of the transitions we experience. These pages offer the concept that there are, once we learn to spot these, <u>landmarks</u> *along the road of transition, both in-life and seeming end-of-life transition.*

- These pages share the idea that *we can <u>harvest</u> our energy and ourselves from our transitions. Energy held in, even locked in, patterns can be freed during transition from previous patterns.*

- These pages suggest that we can *develop* **navigational tools** *to move ourselves, our consciousness-es, through all transitions, including deaths.*

- This book shares the sense that we can ***consciously trigger*** and experience minor and major ***initiation processes*** in our transitions, including in minor and major in-life and end-of life pattern deaths.

- We can each redefine for ourselves what end-of-life death means to us.

CONSCIOUSLY MOVING THROUGH
LIFE'S CHANGES, TRANSITIONS, AND DEATHS

- **End of physical, biological, body life is not necessarily end-of-life along the broader continuum we have the option of seeing once we SEE BEYOND OUR LINE OF SIGHT.**

These and other ideas are shared in this book, to share the possibility, and for many the reality, that we can indeed SEE BEYOND OUR LINE OF SIGHT to ever more CONSCIOUSLY MOVE THROUGH LIFE'S CHANGES, TRANSITIONS, AND DEATHS.

SEEING BEYOND OUR LINE OF SIGHT

PART ONE

Transition Awareness, Transition Management

**CONSCIOUSLY MOVING THROUGH
LIFE'S CHANGES, TRANSITIONS, AND DEATHS**

2
Know Life's Transitional Nature

This book is written for anyone who is undergoing, has undergone, or will undergo a major event, change, or ending. This includes all forms of transition, forms of minor and major change and death of some sort, whether emotional or physical (or conceptual, for that matter). This book is therefore written for everyone.

This includes those who may be experiencing divorce, or being fired, or leaving home, or having one's children leave home. This includes those experiencing abrupt changes or endings such as having one's home collapse in an earthquake, receiving a serious injury, or having something precious stolen.

This also includes those experiencing what are frequently less obvious, more gradual, but definite changes such as: changes in behavioral patterns -- shifting out of a steady or an addictive relationship to a thought pattern, or to a drug, or to a person, or to a behavior.

This also includes those who are outgrowing a stage of life, a philosophy, a religion or another belief system; those who are aging; those who are experiencing having some of their oldest friends die; those who are experiencing the disease process, whether it is temporary, chronic, or "terminal."

Of course, we can include here the concept of dying with which we think we are so familiar: physical death, which is seen by many people as the ultimate of all deaths. Certainly, this book is also written for those experiencing their own and others' actual physical dying and death processes.

Indeed, physical death–the experience of this profound death process, takes many different forms. Physical death, however it is experienced, is in essence the greatest *initiation by transition*.

Physical death presents us a metaphor for in-life endings and deaths, as well as end-of life endings and deaths. Physical death is a model of the small and great deaths, the transitions, that each and every one of us endures. (See the chapters in Part Three of this book: *Physical Death As Transition*.)

You CAN Make It Through

The word "endure" is used here because all in-life as well as end-of-life deaths, all endings, are transitions that can be ever more *consciously navigated*. In this sense, while we cannot change all that is happening around and to us, we CAN affect *our definition and experience of* what is taking place. We CAN move through the transitions we face with increasing degrees of understanding of the process itself.

> **We can fuel our own consciousness**
> **to hold its focus, its SELF,**
> **even in challenging processes.**

On some level, you already know this. You have already been through many profound transitions in your lifetime. You have been born, you have walked your first steps. You likely had a first day of school, saw your early childhood end, became an adolescent, fell in love for the first time, finished school, left home, got hired, got married, and or maybe have been laid off or fired, divorced, or have mourned the death of a family member or friend, or have experienced some other life change.

Transition Replaces Death And Dying Concepts

Of course, not all of these are considered entirely sorrowful, unpleasant, or difficult experiences. Why then, can many of these events, changes, endings, minor and major deaths, these *transition experiences*, feel at least a little bit like death?

Because **all changes**, shifts in and endings of passages, and shifts in and endings of the patterns we form as we move through these passages, are

**transitions from
one state of being to another**.

Whether these seem to be "good" or "bad" transitions, these are all, in a sense, endings of previous passages and their patterns (or sub-patterns).

As passages are by nature passages from one place or situation to another, all these are passages,

**transitions,

into a new state.**

SEEING BEYOND OUR LINE OF SIGHT

Here is where death of a passage and its patterns is *actually far more than an ending with nothing to follow it*.[4]

Stretch The Meaning Of The Word, Death

We must allow ourselves to stretch the meaning of the word "death" this way in order to fully understand and appreciate passages in, events in, even stages of, even cycles of, life. Certainly, we feel changes and transitions. Frequently, these are growing pains. Sometimes these are the pains of not growing while needing to. Sometimes these are the pains of growing in a way that is not needed, or perhaps even detrimental.

Changes, endings, in-life as well as end-of-life deaths, are *transitional experiences*. Some of these transitional experiences can be somewhat unsettling, at times even somewhat disturbing, and

---

[4] For discussion of the *power that patterns have to hold themselves in place*, even to cause us to feel the challenging, intense, even at times death-like effects of trying to break out of these patterns---such as withdrawals from problem patterns (e.g. drug addictions, gambling addictions, other problem addictions, or perhaps even dangerous relationships), see the NAVIGATING LIFE'S STUFF Books listed on the reading list at the end of this present book.

or even frightening, especially when we cannot define these as otherwise.

We can learn to see and experience what we think of as only difficult experiences as more than difficult, to use these *transitional experiences* to further develop our awareness of ourselves and of our options.

Death Is Birth
And There May Be Labor Pains

Pain is more than just a four letter word. Pain is a sensation that seems to hurt. Anyone who has experienced intense pain knows that the *sensation of pain* is very real, about as real as any experience we ever encounter. Some pain can even be so intense that it can threaten the will to live.

Pain takes many forms. Some pain is called pain and is obvious. Some pain is vague and undefined. Some pain may be experienced without being recognized as pain.

Pain cannot be denied. The suffering so many of us have experienced is all too real. And, it can be quite challenging amidst a painful experience to focus on ideas regarding transcendence of this pain. It can also be quite difficult during a painful experience to focus on survival itself. Here is where the idea of training oneself all through life, so as to be ever more able to maintain focus during all transitions, minor and major, is valuable.

**It is never too late to begin training yourself,
your consciousness ...
... to consciously survive transitions and deaths.**

**We can begin with the subtle
rethinking of transition and death offered in this book.**[5]

By survival here, I am referring to the *survival of the self*, the survival of the *personal consciousness*, the survival which I have defined in other books in this series. (Note that the term, *sur- vival*, suggests there is life above, beyond, the life we see, in that the "sur" is above or beyond, and the "vival" is life.)

Here, the idea that we have a *personal consciousness* that perhaps can, *if we wish to have it do so,* choose to *survive*, is

---

[5] Exercises for this training are provided in other books in this series such as Volume 3 of this series, UNVEILING THE HIDDEN INSTINCT, and Volume 4 of this series, HOW TO DIE AND SURVIVE. See reading list at the end of this present book.

KEY. Already we can see that the *personal consciousness* can choose to be reaching beyond the given LINE OF SIGHT.

[Note that meditation and other processes (such as medicinal and even psychoactive treatments) may be helpful in some circumstances. However, any process including those removing us from our own un-mediated, and un-drugged where possible, *fully conscious contact* with and control of our own consciousness--does not entirely prepare us for *consciously maintaining our awareness during intense transitions and deaths.*]

Pain Carries Information

Pain itself carries information from us to ourselves. Pain itself can be understood differently, reframed to help map and manage, to help *travel painful sensations into higher states.*

Those Readers who have given birth may know the feeling of labor pains – of pain cycling in and out, of traveling through layers or rings of pain which quicken over time until a baby is born. Some Readers who have been through dying processes and lived to describe these, also have described these processes as parallel to labor pain experiences.

Death Is Transition

Think of any ending or death process, including physical death, as giving birth to yourself, and what may register as emotional and physical pain as labor pain.

Now there can be a *direction to the pain*, and an outcome to the process. This outcome is a birth into a new reality: your new reality. This can be, *you have the option of choosing* to have this be, the *deliverance of your personal consciousness to a new state of awareness and existence.*

The outcome is moving your awareness beyond the seeming end point on the seeming LINE OF SIGHT: The outcome is moving onto a *never ending continuum.* **On this continuum, the destination is the <u>transit</u> itself:** *the transition is ongoing, the life is ongoing.*

(This never ending continuum is defined and discussed in later chapters of this book, and in other books in this KEYS TO CONSCIOUSNESS AND SURVIVAL SERIES, as being the *continuum of consciousness.*)

Moving Into A New Pattern Of Being

Again, death, the death of anything – of your emotional pattern, your behavioral habit, your state of mind, your stage of life, your way of life, your view of the world, your physical body–is a transition, a passage. What we might describe here as a "survived" death is a *transition of our awareness* onto the *continuum of existence*. We can make this transition as consciously as we choose.

BEING AWARE OF
AND FURTHER DEVELOPING
OUR OWN *ONGOING* PATTERN OF BEING
IS CENTRAL FOR US,
AND IS KEY IN OUR
CONSCIOUS SURVIVAL OF TRANSITIONS IN BOTH
IN-LIFE AND SEEMING END-OF-LIFE
ENDINGS AND DEATHS.

For a new *pattern of being* to be formed, a previous pattern of being is being re-formed, transitioned, moved beyond. Patterns, even ***patterns of being***, are always in transition.

And, of course, not all transitions are painful or traumatic. Every day begins and ends, cycles through day and night. Every breath you take begins and ends, cycles through an inhale-exhale

process. Every step you take has a beginning and an ending. Yet, it is also followed by a (conceptual or actual) next step. Everything you do has a beginning and an ending, and then a next beginning, a next step or transition, to it.

We tend to move right through many transitions, many changes, many endings and beginnings, too busy to realize that we have just survived one of an infinite number of transitions we undergo every single day. We also tend to pay little attention to the many other, and the many far larger, transitions, patterns, cycles, we are living within and around.

Tuning in to what is taking place is KEY in reading the information and signs always present in the patterns we are moving through. This is a KEY awareness in CONSCIOUSLY MOVING THROUGH LIFE'S CHANGES, TRANSITIONS, AND DEATHS.

**CONSCIOUSLY MOVING THROUGH
LIFE'S CHANGES, TRANSITIONS, AND DEATHS**

3
You CAN Ever More Consciously Navigate Transition

We may not feel we have time to *consciously navigate* every single transition we undergo every single minute of our lives. However, we can incorporate ever increasing awareness, ever increasing consciousness, into any activity we want to be more aware of. For example, ever more conscious breathing, ever more conscious relating, even behaviors such as ever more conscious spending--all minor and major levels of *ever more conscious behavior and awareness* are possible on all fronts.

Strengthen Awareness

Recall the old adage, "use it or lose it." Indeed, even the power of the awareness, of <u>our</u> awareness, can and must be exercised to maximize its capabilities. Awareness is like a muscle, one that can be strengthened and trained with exercise.

Practicing being increasingly aware, ever more conscious, further develops and helps strengthen the consciousness. This practicing can prepare the self, the awareness, the personal consciousness, for times when *being ever more consciously aware can indeed help navigate a challenging experience.*

Awakening The Metacognition

Basically, with this practice, we are training our mental functions, even our awareness functions, including our cognitive functions, to enhance themselves. We are expanding our awareness to reach into our mind's *metacognitive* levels.

Metacognition is KEY in our ever further developing our awareness. What is metacognition? Think of this as the process of *thinking about thinking*. We can become ever more in touch with our thought processes and our thought process**ings**.

Metacognition is indeed *thinking about thinking* -- basically the meta- or overarching level of thinking itself.

As so much of what goes on in our brains and minds is taking place out of our *conscious awareness*, there is so much we have little conscious say in. However, we can gain ever more conscious say in what goes on in our minds and brains as we consciously develop and interact with our own personal metacognition.

The concept of *metacognition* is not as difficult as it may sound. In fact, we are using our metacognitive processes all the time. In this sense, we are already quite adept at metacognition. Our minds process information and then *information about this information* on a continuous basis.

For the most part, we are unaware of this constant work we are doing to detect, process, and respond to external and internal data and stimuli. We just see, hear, taste, smell, touch, and then respond, all without thinking about the massive amount of electro-biochemical translations being made every single millisecond.

Our brains form higher mental functions, even executive controls, to manage – to identify, organize, retain, learn from, and respond to – the stream of incoming (and interactively coming) stimulation we are constantly receiving. This *super* or *supra* level of information processing we do is the executive control our brains are engaging in, our *metacognitive processing*, which functions virtually invisibly, generally beneath our radar.

There is such great power there beneath our own *mental radar*, sitting there without our noticing it. We are thus at the mercy of what we do not consciously know about ourselves, that is, unless ...

WE CONSCIOUSLY
CALL
OUR OWN ATTENTION
TO OUR OWN
METACOGNITIVE PROCESSES.

Meet Your Metacognition

So, meet your metacognition, say hello to your higher, including your executive level, cognitive functions. *Own your metacognition*: talk to it, wake it up, train it, help it help you *to go conscious, to go very conscious.*

This *conscious contact with ourselves, with the workings of our minds/brains*, brings us further into the role of *conscious navigator of ourselves*, of our transitions, of our in-life and end-of-life processes and their patterns.

SEEING BEYOND OUR LINE OF SIGHT

This *conscious contact* allows us to make our processes, (which we are constantly undergoing), far more productive for us.[6]

Conscious Navigation

When we face a challenging or painful transition, its *conscious and metacognitive navigation* can be immensely valuable.

**It is how you move through,
ever more consciously navigate,
a transition
that will set the stage for your next beginning.**

**Entry into any transition,
whether it be minor or major,
or physical death itself,
and management of any of these transitions,
is most effective
when conducted
as consciously as possible.**

---

[6] See the books on this navigation in the KEYS TO CONSCIOUSNESS AND SURVIVAL SERIES: first see: NAVIGATING LIFE'S STUFF: DYNAMICS OF PERSONAL CHANGE, BOOK ONE and then NAVIGATING LIFE'S STUFF: DYNAMICS OF PERSONAL CHANGE, BOOK TWO.

CONSCIOUSLY MOVING THROUGH
LIFE'S CHANGES, TRANSITIONS, AND DEATHS

The more you understand the process, the *great adventure of transition itself*, the more you can use the experience to consciously, with your full attention at work upon it--create your own understanding, your own definition, of the next phase of your life, of your SELF.

You can consciously choose to

**SEE BEYOND
YOUR LINE OF SIGHT.**

You can *design* your next mental, emotional, and spiritual reality.[7] Again, while we cannot control everything that happens to us, around us, and within us, we can have increasing say in how we *experience* what happens.

**We can also gain
more conscious involvement
in the options we have for
our navigation and survival of transitions.**

---

[7] Note that the use of the term, *spiritual*, in this book refers to the spirit of the person, and yes, for some Readers, also the spirit of life. Readers will determine for themselves what this term, *spiritual*, means to them. Also note that this book does not speak to any one particular religious orientation. Nor does this book require of Readers a religious orientation. Rather, this material is written for everyone, of all world views, of all orientations.

Recognizing Transition

Death, in any form, in-life and seeming end-of-life, is indeed a great adventure of the SELF. This is always a challenging and remarkable journey every time you take it.

No two transitions or deaths are the same; however, the passage we call transition or death has characteristics that can be identified again and again.

Learning to consciously recognize these characteristics, these *landmarks along the road of transition*, will ease your passage, will enhance the richness of your experience, will contribute to your survival as a consciousness, and will determine the:

**the richness of the harvest –
you take**

**as you move through
transitions including deaths.**[8]

---

[8] See Volumes 4, 11, and 14 in this KEYS TO CONSCIOUSNESS AND SURVIVAL SERIES, the HOW TO DIE AND SURVIVE books.

CONSCIOUSLY MOVING THROUGH
LIFE'S CHANGES, TRANSITIONS, AND DEATHS

You CAN Harvest Pain And Transition For Conscious Initiation

And you indeed can *harvest* your transitions and deaths. Your harvest can be as abundant as you wish it to be. You can learn as much as you choose to during any transition you undergo.

You can harvest increased awareness, expanded consciousness, a strengthened, fortified, *quickened self*, from the process of transition, from every process of transition whether minor or major.

You can re-think, transform, your experience of the **transition process**. You can transform it from what at times may feel to be a process through which you are aimlessly and hopelessly tumbling, into *an ever more conscious process, even an initiation*. You can transform your journey, and your <u>*self*</u> in the process.

Again, the situation itself, what is taking place in the physical world, on the physical plane, may or may not be amendable.

However, your experience, *your conscious experience of the situation, even of the generally unseen energetic details of the situation*, can become increasingly more aware. You can become ever more adept at navigating the process of the transition you are undergoing. (Refer to the EXERCISE in *General Transition Awareness* at the end of this chapter, titled, *Sensitizing To Landmarks Along The Path Of Transition*.)

On Pain In Transition

Again, this is not to deny any emotional and physical discomfort and pain that may be experienced. We all know pain, some of us more directly and intensely than others.

Pain cannot and should not be denied.

Pain in various forms can be present in various types of trying experiences. Those of us, which is most everyone, if not everyone, who have experienced pain know that pain can be distracting, demanding, even can be dominating, at times almost defeating. It is essential during such an experience to continue to, even to ever more, contact one's personal awareness and thus consciousness.

CONSCIOUSLY MOVING THROUGH
LIFE'S CHANGES, TRANSITIONS, AND DEATHS

Holding on to that personal awareness, to one's consciousness, even when in pain, can be a **KEY** *navigation tool.*

Given that emotional and or physical pain is present, can we put the *experience of pain* to work? Can we find a way to ever more consciously navigate our pain experience to have this experience be useful in the: deepening of the awareness, of the knowledge, of the aware consciousness, of the person experiencing the pain (either directly or indirectly by witnessing it).

**Can the consciousness
speak to itself ever more
as it navigates pain?**

Pain Is More

Pain wears many faces and is not always called pain.

Pain hurts. And pain does far more than hurt. Both emotional and physical pain call our attention to the fact that something is taking place. Pain can be a sign of a need for change, or of a hindrance to change, or of change itself. Pain is a message from us to ourselves. Yet, reading pain is a challenge.

SEEING BEYOND OUR LINE OF SIGHT

Moving through pain can be an even greater challenge. The *pain pattern or program* (which I have defined in depth in other books in this series) *frequently does not want to release us from itself. Once caught in a pain cycle, this pain can be difficult to leave. Where can we go to work with this pain?*

However we address the pain we feel, we can imagine we can move, or we can actually move, our consciousness beyond this physical body pain, into another dimension of ourselves, BEYOND OUR LINE OF SIGHT. (See the sections on DE-SOMATIZATION in the books, UNVEILING THE HIDDEN INSTINCT, and also, HOW TO DIE AND SURVIVE.)

This is *not* to say that: we simply physically leave our physical bodies and thus the physical pain behind, all in a magical way. This *is* to say that: we can shift the focus of our awareness, of our *aware consciousness*, for a time, to another dimension of ourselves. (See the book, UNVEILING THE HIDDEN INSTINCT, for further definition of the *aware consciousness*, and also for exercises in *shifting the focus of the consciousness* to beyond physical body states.)

CONSCIOUSLY MOVING THROUGH
LIFE'S CHANGES, TRANSITIONS, AND DEATHS

While change can seem to hurt, while some change can definitely hurt, so can not changing when change is needed. *Resisting transition can seem as painful as the transition being resisted.* We may be stuck and need to move through a situation–need to move into what I elsewhere define in depth as *transit mode,* and even *conscious transit mode.* (Again, see other books in this series for details on this *transit mode.*)

Understanding what is taking place when we feel caught or stuck or trapped in a situation or sensation such as pain can allow us to ever more consciously read and navigate this situation.

Understanding that <u>the experience itself is the situation</u> even more than the situation is the situation, is KEY.

Returning to pain for a moment:

Yes, pain carries information. We have developed the pain sensation to give ourselves what can be essential information. Think of the child touching the hot stove. It burns. The pain sensation may be saying do not touch a very hot thing again as this can hurt.

SEEING BEYOND OUR LINE OF SIGHT

The question is, when does pain become so dominating that it is no longer serving its original function, no longer giving us essential information to help us survive? We must be watchful for times when this is the case, when pain is not functioning as it was designed to do.

While detaching from pain is frequently quite difficult, temporarily moving one's focus out of the physical body, the physical self, enough to work on the pain from another conceptual level of awareness can be valuable, even KEY.[9]

Moving The Awareness To Another Level Of Itself

Here is the awareness, the *aware consciousness*, moving itself, moving its focus, into other dimensions of itself, whether it remains linked to the physical body or leaves it. Here is the *aware consciousness expanding itself along the continuum of consciousness.*

I have elsewhere defined in depth the notion that the consciousness, specifically what I have defined as the <u>aware</u>

---

[9] See again other books in this series for exercises regarding moving to *nonphysical levels of awareness*, such as the books, UNVEILING THE HIDDEN INSTINCT and also HOW TO DIE AND SURVIVE.

consciousness, may have the option of surviving even independent of the physical body. (See the *Series Foreword* at the opening of this present book, and also other books in this series, when ready to examine this matter in great depth and to find exercises for further and specifically developing the *aware* consciousness.[10])

We can SEE <u>BEYOND</u> OUR LINE OF SIGHT to move ourselves (our minds, our focus, our sense of self) <u>past the boundaries</u> of the physical dimension of our existence. We can move ourselves and our sense of our lives to our own *continuum of consciousness* that we can define for ourselves. (See later chapters in this book for definition and discussion of this **continuum of consciousness**.)

Recognizing that we have or can develop this option for ourselves is essential. We can begin consciously knowing this every day we live.

We can then be maintaining, even in our daily 3-D physical plane lives, an *extended sense of location along an extended*

---

[10] See especially the exercises in UNVEILING THE HIDDEN INSTINCT.

SEEING BEYOND OUR LINE OF SIGHT

continuum that reaches beyond what our physical plane LINE OF SIGHT shows us. We can choose to live along our own *continuum of consciousness* where we can *be*, where we can survive, in the form of our awareness, of our aware consciousness.

We can choose to further locate, or further expand, along this continuum during all in-life and so-called end-of life transitions. Now end-of-life transitions are no longer conceptually, or perhaps even actually (depending upon our preparation for this) confined to end-of-life. In other words:

We can survive as who we truly are, both here and BEYOND.

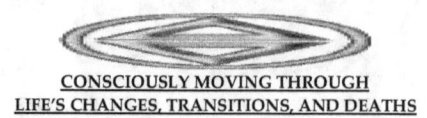
**CONSCIOUSLY MOVING THROUGH
LIFE'S CHANGES, TRANSITIONS, AND DEATHS**

Sensitizing To Landmarks Along The Path Of Transition

EXERCISE: General Transition Awareness

This exercise suggests that we can *fine tune ourselves, sensitize ourselves*, to even the less distinct yet still important elements of the transitions we experience. These questions are general suggestions to us, and to our *awareness functions*.

This process invites our minds to increase our *transition awareness*, to continuously build on this awareness as per our *personal consciousness*.

These questions suggest we can alert ourselves to both these obvious and also these more subtle aspects of the *transition experiences* we are engaged in. We certainly do know when we are experiencing some of the following listed below. And we certainly do not know or realize we are experiencing all of these listed here.

We are frequently deeply into a process, a transition, before we see that it has started or continued or changed or completed or moved into other transition processes. We can however, alert ourselves to what is taking place and where we are. In so doing, we can *fine tune our awareness functions* to be ever more aware, ever more conscious, during our transition processes, which is during every moment of our lives.

CONSCIOUSLY MOVING THROUGH
LIFE'S CHANGES, TRANSITIONS, AND DEATHS

FIVE TRANSITION AWARENESS EXERCISE STEPS

ONE: Note Transition Stage
What transition stage does this appear to be?
What part of the transition does this situation,
change, event, process, feel to be?

1) Is this a transition lead-in stage, AND OR IS THIS
2) An ongoing transition process stage, AND OR IS THIS
3) A transition climax stage (if any), AND OR IS THIS,
4) A transition completion stage (if any), AND OR IS THIS
5) A transition moving into a next transition stage, AND OR IS THIS
6) A transition merging with other transition stages, AND OR IS THIS
7) Another transition process stage?
8) Or, does this transition appear to be permanent or ongoing, or never ending?
9) Or, are the answers to the above unclear at this time?
10) Add your own questions as per **transition stage awareness** here.

TWO: Note Transition Pattern Signs and Sensations

Note obvious and specific, and also even vague and unclear, signs and sensations indicating that a transition process is or may be taking place.

Note any signs and sensations such as but not limited to these:
1) Sense that a pattern of emotion or thought or behavior has emerged.
2) Sense that a pattern is dominating a situation.
3) Sense that you are experiencing, or living, a pattern (such as a behavioral cycle, perhaps even a habit or an addiction, or an emotional cycle).
4) Sense when you are feeling (or being) caught or trapped or stuck in a pattern.
5) Sense when your energy is being affected by a pattern.
6) Sense when your energy appears to build up, or distort, or diminish.
7) Sense when there is a build-up of symptoms and signs suggesting that you are suspended within a pattern – perhaps seemingly endlessly.
8) Sense when there is a build up of stress, anxiety.
9) Sense when there is a build up of emotional issues.
10) Sense when there is a build up of physical issues.
11) Sense when energy appears to shift or move into an out of control mode.
12) Become aware of the above and other signs and sensations not listed here.
13) Add your own questions regarding **transition signs and sensations** to this list.

CONSCIOUSLY MOVING THROUGH
LIFE'S CHANGES, TRANSITIONS, AND DEATHS

THREE: Note Ongoing Transition Elements

Many elements of transition processes become more visible to us once we fine tune our own awareness to these.

We can begin now, even in daily life, to further sensitize ourselves to elements of transition.

Note any sensations such as but not limited to these:

1) Sense building of forces and factors.
2) Sense no exit situations.
3) Sense disorientation or confusion.
4) Sense when you are unclear on how to proceed.
5) Sense obstacles and blocking factors.
6) Sense what appear to be openings to something unclear.
7) Sense openings to alternative transition pathways.
8) Sense windows of opportunity.
9) Sense safe exits.
10) Become aware of other frequently vague yet present elements in the transition reality you are moving through or caught in.
11) Add your own **transition elements** to this list.

FOUR: Note Navigation Issues, Awareness-es
Note any sensations such as but not limited to these:
1) Bring awareness to sensations.
   Sense the presence of passages through sensation patterns.
2) Detect energy situations.
   Watch for openings into passages through energy situations.
3) See variations in one's attention functions.
   Find passages through attention situations.
4) See variations in one's decision making functions.
   Find passages through decision making situations.
5) Imagine you are moving through a complex map or puzzle or obstacle course.
   Watch for factors, forces, elements offering opportunity to move.
6) Be aware of factors and forces blocking, slowing, detouring your positive progress through this transition.
   Sense the presence of these issues via imagination, visualization, sensory, or other awareness functions.
7) Add your own additional **navigation issues and awareness-es** to this list.

FIVE: Note Co-occurring Transitions

It is important to note your awareness of other transitions also taking place parallel to, nearby, within, instead of, or in other ways around your own transition processes. The following are just some of the many examples.

Be aware of and sensitize yourself to the effects of:

1) Another transition process you are also in the process of.
2) Another transition process someone else is also in the process of.
3) Another transition process that is within your present transition process.
4) Another transition process that your present transition process exists within.
5) Another transition process subsuming or swallowing or otherwise dominating your transition process.
6) Add your own ideas of transition processes that may be occurring at the same time.
7) Add your own ideas of **co-occurring transition processes** that may be affecting your transition processes.

SEEING BEYOND OUR LINE OF SIGHT

The above list of Five Transition Awareness Exercise Steps is just a starting point. These self check-ins open the brain and mind to ever increasing *transition awareness*. Continue to define and refine your own list of *transition navigation check-ins, signs, sensations, landmarks.*

Every transition sign, sensation, and landmark you alert your mind to will have corresponding brain activity, micro level brain changes -- just as every sensation, idea, thought, and thought pattern does. The goal here is to become ever more *consciously aware* of the obvious and the subtle in-life transition experiences.

This training of the aware consciousness can continue through all in-life transition processes. This is building the strength of the aware consciousness to remain ever more aware and alert through all transitions, including transitions where *maintaining the <u>continuity of the personal consciousness</u> is KEY in survival.*

4
Consciously Entering Into Transition: The Idea of Transition Management

Life is a continuous process of transition. Every moment changes are taking place. We may or may not see these changes. We may or may not be conscious of all of these changes, however these are always underway. We are always affected on some level by these.

Transition Awareness

Sometimes ongoing transitions are difficult to detect. In fact, there are times when things seem *not* to be changing or moving, when situations feel to be in holding patterns, whether healthy or unhealthy or neutral. While many of our transitions and their patterns make their presences clear to us, many others (including co-patterns, sub-patterns, and underlying patterns) are lurking beneath our *conscious radar*.

**CONSCIOUSLY MOVING THROUGH
LIFE'S CHANGES, TRANSITIONS, AND DEATHS**

Sensitizing ourselves to even the most difficult to detect patterns we are living with and within can allow us to more *consciously navigate our lives* (as I have discussed in depth in the NAVIGATING LIFE'S STUFF Books).

We can learn to feel and see signs and characteristics of the various patterns we are moving within and through. (*Refer to the* EXERCISE in General Transition Awareness *at the end of the previous chapter, titled,* Sensitizing To Landmarks Along The Path Of Transition.)

Some Transitions Feel Slow Or Stuck

Some patterns and their *transitional states* have particular characteristics that may feel to be more rigid or dense. We can read the nature of slow and even stuck transitional processes by sensing their, at times, less distinct characteristics.

When we are feeling caught or trapped, in some way stuck, we may need to resolve the pressure or stuck sensation by

consciously entering into, or deeper into, a *more conscious transition navigation process.*[11]

We may realize that we face obstacles and hindrances to *moving productively through particular transition processes.* Recognizing the presence and nature of these frequently invisible obstacles and hindrances can help us be more conscious of what I have elsewhere defined as the *pattern terrain*. This heightened awareness helps us navigate, move, *transition*, through.[12]

This Is About Our Making Contact With Our Own Knowledge

Our *conscious transition management* is empowered by our ever increasing access to our own awareness functions.

---

[11] In depth definition, description, and discussion of *transition navigation* is found in Book One and then Book Two of the NAVIGATING LIFE'S STUFF books. These are Volumes 8 and 9 in this KEYS TO CONSCIOUSNESS AND SURVIVAL SERIES.

[12] See the in-depth definition, discussion, and description of the PATTERN TERRAIN itself and of these hindrances referred to above in the books, NAVIGATING LIFE'S STUFF: DYNAMICS OF PERSONAL CHANGE, Books One and Two.

This is about our making contact with our own largely untapped inner resources, with the virtually hidden deeper workings of our brain and mind, what is right there yet designed to take place under our own radar, in the realm of our sub- and even un- consciousness.

There is a great deal of information there awaiting our discovery. This is *our* information, this information is there in *our* own brains for *us* to contact. The way we are biologically wired has formed a block to our accessing much of what is in there, of what is already ours to know, yet invisible to us.

However, we are approaching a time when we may need to access far more of ourselves than we have been given the key to—given by evolution or biology, or by some other form of design. We have somehow been formed to have a biological brain that handles conscious access to

only a small part of its own knowledge, to only a small part of its rightful access to itself.[13]

Speak To Your Mind

We can continuously sharpen our awareness of the transitions we are moving within and through. We can become ever more aware of the similarities and differences among our various minor and major transitions, such as: the stages of our transition processes, the various characteristics of our transitions -- such as their pace, their intensity, their complexity or simplicity, the amount of stress or pain or other sensations we connect to particular transition experiences or stages of transitions, the way we make it through our various transitions – if we do, and so on.

Some changes, transitions from one situation or condition to another, are relatively easy, and almost unnoticeable. Some changes are a little complex, but nothing too difficult to manage. Other changes present mental, emotional, spiritual, social,

---

[13] This is the central discussion in the Part One and Part Two books of OVERRIDING THE EXTINCTION SCENARIO, Volumes 5 and 6 in this KEYS TO CONSCIOUSNESS AND SURVIVAL SERIES.

financial, even physical challenges. Some changes can be quite difficult, some even grueling.

However, no matter how obvious parts of our transitions are to us, much of our change and transition processes take place far beneath our conscious radar. (What our brain is designed to allow us to know of our transition situations may be only the tip of the iceberg. We are blocked from conscious access to so much information.[14])

How dearly we would like all changes, all transitions from one situation to another, to be as easy and comfortable as possible. And we would like every possible effort, whether psychologically or spiritually or socially or perhaps also financially, or even medically, to be made to help ease these transitions.

Yet, quite often we are left with the most difficult aspects of these situations, these transitions, to manage on our own. No matter what sort of support we may or may not have as we face

---

[14] See again the books, OVERRIDING THE EXTINCTION SCENARIO, Part One and Part Two.

and undergo transitions in our lives, we are on some level undergoing what we are undergoing on our own.

Nothing can deny or take away the personal experience of a situation, a transition, we are facing. While we cannot change all that is happening around and within us, what we can seek to change or affect to some degree is *how we consciously experience and navigate the transitions we undergo.*

Frame The Transition Process

We can ask ourselves: Can we find a way to frame (or <u>RE</u>-frame) our experience as being a process further opening states of mind, further awareness-es, to us? Can we frame the *transition process itself* in a way that we can give it our own personal story, our own personal imprint? We can choose to answer: yes, we can.

Any experience we experience is ours to label, to frame, for ourselves. Holding on to this idea is KEY in moving through even difficult processes. We can tell ourselves how we choose to label our process, how we choose to define what we are going through. We can even define for ourselves our location along our LINE OF SIGHT.

**CONSCIOUSLY MOVING THROUGH
LIFE'S CHANGES, TRANSITIONS, AND DEATHS**

Of course, this may not sound easy or logical in the midst of very difficult situations, those that may be highly stressful, or painful, or perhaps frightening. **Yet, if we can find even a *thread of possibility, a thread of meaning to give ourselves, make an even faint map of what we are going through*, we can begin to gain some sense that we are consciously identifying,** *directing, navigating our experience.*[15]

We can talk to ourselves, to our minds, to our brains, to the metacognition and its executive control of our mind-brains:

> *Brain, mind, I am calling you to me, I am calling you to speak with me. Whether you are my higher self, or my brain's organizing function, or my consciousness itself, whatever you may be or whatever I may think you are, I am calling you to step forward and let me speak to you, which*

---

[15] See exercises for *transition mapping* in books listed in the recommended reading at the end of this present book, such as in Volume 2 in this series, titled, ADVENTURES IN CHANGES, TRANSITIONS, AND DEATHS. Also see mapping and charting exercises in volumes in the FACES OF ADDICTION SERIES, such as the book titled, SEEING THE HIDDEN FACE OF ADDICTION and also TRANSCENDING ADDICTION.

is to speak to ME. I will walk you, myself, through this process as consciously as I can.

Pain Can Be Fuel

This discussion must talk again about emotional, physical, and other pain, including other forms of distress that are in some way painful. Pain can come into play. Pain can be a dominating factor. Pain can almost be defeating.

Whether it be emotional or spiritual or physical, or some other form of pain, or all of these forms of pain together, pain can stand between us and ourselves, between us and hope, even between us and personal peace. (Note: Pain can even slow or complicate a transition. Keep in mind that emotional pain such as depression can register as physical pain, and vice versa.)

One of the greatest challenges during any transition is difficult, painful, sensation such as emotion. Another is physical pain. As noted earlier, pain can even appear to take several forms, or at times to be difficult to categorize. We may register pain in various ways, ranging from non-physical to physical.

However we feel this pain, whatever medical or other treatment may or may not be received, ultimately, the matter is how we navigate this pain. Yes, how our brains, our minds, and our consciousness-es address this pain is a central matter here.

[Note that this book does not speak to medical or even psychological (such as hypnosis) methods of pain management, as these are left to others to discuss. What this book does speak to is *transition management* and *transition navigation*.]

All too frequently, pain can block our conscious contact with our SELVES. And yet, it is this pain itself that can carry information and energy we can use, frequently need to use as we undergo *transitional states*.

**Initiation Into
Conscious Transition
And
Conscious Management Of Transition**

KEY in managing transition is thinking about how to frame, define, move through (navigate) the transition process itself. This can be a *process building the self, the awareness*, to a point where minor and or major …

transformational transition experiences can ever more consciously take place.

Whether it be hidden or obvious, emotional or physical or some other form, pain can be part of, or transformed into something which is part of, an initiation process. Initiation. Yes, initiation into a next phase, a new way of seeing the world, a new self. When navigated as such, pain can carry (or be harvested for) its *initiation potential*.

This in no way says pain should be purposefully experienced. Rather, this says, ever more consciously navigating the pain experience can open new avenues of self.

Initiation can be entry into an ever more conscious level of one's transition process, and of learning from this transition process. This **conscious initiation** represents an increase in **navigation awareness**, consciously drawing the attention of the mind-brain to the sensations of moving through transition.

This involves an increase in, and expansion of, what I have elsewhere defined as: the *conscious awareness* and the *aware*

consciousness. (See the book, UNVEILING THE HIDDEN INSTINCT.)

This book is about *conscious initiation* into *conscious transition*, and into *conscious management of transition*. Where initiation offers this, then this is indeed a valuable initiation.

Translating Pain Into Initiation Into Increased Awareness

However pain registers, what ever form the pain takes, pain makes its presence known. Whether we feel the hurt or the hurt hits us below our conscious radar, on a subconscious level, we are affected.

Again, pain takes a range of forms, from emotional to physical to mental to psychic to other forms. We must never trivialize or minimize the pain experience, or any stress, suffering, demoralization, that may be experienced as part of this. Each pain experience translates differently, and each individual person has his or her own experience.

Pain must be understood for what it carries, what it constitutes, what its messages may be. While we cannot always

stop or even reduce pain itself, we can begin to see how the pain experience is itself demanding, drawing, distorting, holding, our energy, and that this is energy we need for ourselves and our transitions.

Therefore, some of the pain can be drawn upon as fuel, when some of the pain is viewed this way. With skilled guidance, some of the pain experience can be harvested for growth, survival, and transcendence.[16] In this sense, even a painful pattern ending, or pattern transition of some form, can be viewed

---

[16] Readers are urged to always check the professional qualifications, licenses, training, and experience of those who offer such guidance. Not only check the professional qualifications, but also consider the application of these qualifications by the professionals being considered, while selecting professionals who can truly provide guidance and assistance with transition experiences. Far too many persons certified in various very important and useful areas, for example EMDR and hypnosis to name just two, are not necessarily proficient in guiding transition processes with the level of sensitivity called for in this book. *This is in no way a criticism* of these and other credentials, rather a suggestion that these credentials themselves do not guarantee the awareness involved in guiding persons through in-life and seeming end-of-life transition experiences, and in guiding these persons in their consideration of the *continuum of consciousness* itself (as defined in later chapters of this book).

as a *powerful initiation*. We carry within us the KEY to unlock this power, *our power*.

On some level we are aware of this. Yet, few people consciously prepare for this *initiation-by-pattern-death*, or any of their other seemingly smaller *initiation-by-transition*, or other *initiation-by-living-death* adventures.

Again, we are often quite naturally and rightfully pain avoidant, thus not consciously addressing emotional, physical, and other pain this way. We can however, begin to talk to our mind, to our brain, even to our consciousness itself. We can begin to *dialog with ourselves, with our aware consciousness*. We can consciously communicate with ourselves regarding our desire to ever more consciously navigate difficult, even painful changes, transitions, in-life and seeming end-of-life deaths.

Detect Blocks To
Conscious Transition Management

We are frequently quite naturally avoidant of conscious *transition options*. What goes on within us that renders us avoidant of transition or at least avoidant of ever more conscious transition?

SEEING BEYOND OUR LINE OF SIGHT

One of the reasons for this avoidance is that we are, as noted earlier, quite naturally and logically avoidant of great emotional or physical pain, and avoidant of seemingly great unknowns that suggest pain or the risk of pain. This avoidance is frequently relayed to us by our brains, for example in the form of states of mind such as: avoidance behavior itself, and or distraction and concentration problems; and or vague, free floating anxiety; and or specific anxiety; and or vague free floating worry; and or in something appearing under the specific label of *fear* itself.

Pain sensations themselves can tend to be processed by our brains as negative feedback or holding patterns that do not readily release us. Once a *pain pattern* takes hold, that pattern can dominate our experience and even our conscious movement through this experience.

Pain patterning itself contains and utilizes (and can even control) energy we may want for other purposes. Seeing pain as a *pocket of energy* we may choose to move is KEY in ever more consciously managing transition processes. Releasing ourselves

from hindrances and blocks to effective transition management can empower us along the way.

Seeking sudden release from pain itself, at times any release that is found to be some degree of release, is frequently the driver, the motivation. We can understand and mobilize even emotional and physical pain to drive us, move us onward. *While this may not eliminate the pain, it can **mobilize the pain experience for us**. **In so doing, we can further activate our awareness functions.***

Obstacles To Surviving Transition Well

We do not consciously plan for many of life's changes and transitions, except perhaps to: buy insurance; write wills, trusts, and medical directives; and maybe pray for some kind of salvation or direction. However, it is not only fear which keeps us from consciously preparing for initiation by in-life or seeming end-of-life transition.

States of mind that can interfere with conscious transition management can include fear, as well as deep programming, lack of information, and taboo.

SEEING BEYOND OUR LINE OF SIGHT

Fear is one of the states of mind that can keep us from knowing how to plan for, manage, take control of, successfully endure, and harvest our in-life and also seeming end-of-life ending, dying, changing, transitioning, processes.

Next to fear is our *deep programming*, the deep behavioral and energetic patterning to which we are programmed to be addicted. This programing builds within us the *pattern addiction* tendencies we all carry, and for good reason.[17]

And next to pattern addiction is *lack of information*. We have not been taught the true nature of, as well as similarities and differences between, in-life death, and seeming end-of-life death. Even what the death transition is (**or has the potential of becoming**) has not been made as clear as it can be. Perhaps we have either denied ourselves, or have been denied, many truths

---

[17] See my discussion on our being programmed to be both positively and negatively addicted in books where I develop this notion (such as in the book, SEEING THE HIDDEN FACE OF ADDICTION: DETECTING AND CONFRONTING THIS INVASIVE PRESENCE). See also the book where I detail the nature of *pattern addiction:* NAVIGATING LIFE'S STUFF: DYNAMICS OF PERSONAL CHANGE, Book One.

about our existences. Or perhaps we have not been allowed to truly wonder.

And, beyond these states of mind is the overall looming social state of mind -- the *cultural taboos and laws* we may have developed and enacted against learning how to ever more consciously undergo change, transition, in-life and so called end-of-life death. We have been, to a great degree, blocked from our own *conscious access* to our own *continuum of consciousness*.

Thus, our awareness of what our options are as per the *continuum of our own consciousness* is limited or even blocked.[18] That we can choose to extend our known LINE OF SIGHT may not be fully explained. That we have a right to extend our own LINE OF SIGHT may not even be suggested.

You Travel Transition

You can and do have some say in how you manage and navigate the mental, emotional, and physical experiences you may undergo in your transitions, physical or otherwise. You can

---

[18] See the discussion in Volumes 4, 11, and 14 of this series, the HOW TO DIE AND SURVIVE books.

have some say in how you view these experiences, how you define these experiences, how you ever more consciously navigate these experiences.

Dare we ask why most of us do not know the full extent of this say we have? Consider the possibility that we may have been denied the truth about death – perhaps by belief systems, by education, by leaders, by those among us who know, even by evolution itself.

Why deny us truth?

Because we as individuals, and as whole populations, are likely to be much easier to control if we spend our energy worrying about, avoiding, or denying the notion of surviving profound transition such as death. We are much easier to control through our fears, our pattern addictions, our lacks of information, our explicit and implicit cultural, religious, and legislative *taboos against knowing*.[19]

---

[19] See other books in this KEYS TO CONSCIOUSNESS AND SURVIVAL SERIES for discussion of taboos re, and blocks to, this knowing, such as Volume 3 titled, UNVEILING THE HIDDEN INSTINCT, and also Volumes 4, 11, and 14, the HOW TO DIE AND SURVIVE books.

CONSCIOUSLY MOVING THROUGH
LIFE'S CHANGES, TRANSITIONS, AND DEATHS

We are already, on some level, aware that we are beings who exist along our *continuum of consciousness*. Bringing this understanding to the forefront now, being ever more conscious of what this means and what our options are as we move along this continuum, is our option, is our right, and may at some point even be very necessary to our survival.[20]

We can consciously unlock the doors to our own access to what is already ours: (a) our own identity as not simply biological beings but also as beings who are a **species of consciousness**; and (b) our own access to our own continuum of consciousness; and thus to (c) our right to exist all along this continuum and therefore our....

RIGHT TO SURVIVE.

---

[20] See books in this series for in depth discussion of our survival options: Volumes 5 and 6, the OVERRIDING THE EXTINCTION SCENARIO books.

5
Moving Beyond Limits
We Are Told Exist

Were each and every one of us encouraged to ever more *consciously navigate transitions*, we could become a still more aware and alert species. We could be ever more powerful as individuals and as a collective life force. Whatever forces (from within us or outside us) hold us captive to a restricted LINE OF SIGHT will be severely threatened when we become ever more conscious masters of our own transition processes.

In other words, the fears and limitations we feel (and have grown to believe are actual) may simply be part of the brainwashing we have endured for so long.

We need not be prisoners of false limitations, and of false definitions of who we are, once we have the KEY to the exit from the land of narrow beliefs, from the restricted LINE OF SIGHT. And we do have the KEY.

Mastering Transition Processes

I am inviting you to become exactly this: captain of your own transition processes, your own minor and major changes, endings, in-life and seeming end-of-life deaths. These are all transitions. In essence, all processes are transitions. All life is a series of transition processes.

Ever more consciously becoming alert to *transitions* will enable you to further master your life. After all, we are always: breathing in and breathing out and breathing in; waking up and going to sleep and waking up; leaning forward, even falling forward, to take a step and move forward, then taking that next step. Change is a constant state. All within and around us is always in transition. And so is our world.

Rethink The Concept Of Death

Rethink the concept of death for yourself and for all Humanity. Your – our -- survival, even our freedom of will, depends upon the spreading of this awareness: We have a right to *consciously occupy* our *continuum of consciousness* at all times while living in our physical bodies and while living BEYOND the physical body's LINE OF SIGHT. We can choose

to develop our ability to survive death as we locate ourselves along the *continuum of consciousness*. (This continuum of consciousness is defined in later chapters of this book.) We can choose to define ourselves as what and who we truly are: *a **species** of consciousness*.[21]

You will grow to understand this on a deep level as you explore what you find in this book, and the awareness this material spawns–revives--in your soul.[22] These ideas about transition and death processes will flow gently into your consciousness and metacognitive intelligence, and will allow you to take these ideas as lightly or as profoundly as you wish -- as you feel ready to.

These ideas will actually identify, refine, and clarify themselves for us as we grow more conscious of them. These

---

[21] Definition and discussion of ourselves as *Humanity, a species of consciousness* is contained in other books in this series such as UNVEILING THE HIDDEN INSTINCT.

[22] Further and in depth definitions and discussions of the *conscious awareness* in moving us through transitions, even dimensions, of life and death, are provided in Volume 3, UNVEILING THE HIDDEN INSTINCT: UNDERSTANDING OUR INTERDIMENSIONAL SURVIVAL AWARENESS.

ideas will be flowing to and from the population or the species mind, to and from the collective consciousness, and to and from your own personal subconsciousness and consciousness.

You wake up, someone else wakes up, the next one wakes up, the population of us wakes up. This book, and you, will help fuel this survival process, awakening essential KEY understandings of transition, change, and death we all carry.

Ultimately, our survival as a *species of consciousness* is up to us. We can claim our rightful place along the *continuum of consciousness* where we already do live. This requires our understanding who and what we actually are.

SEEING BEYOND OUR LINE OF SIGHT

IMPORTANT NOTE

Let's be clear here. Nothing in this book advocates suicide. Many persons' suicides are understandably conducted in a state of desperation, or of extreme confusion, or perhaps quite rationally to exit severe pain.

While such desperation, confusion, pain are for so many truly nearly or entirely unbearable, other options must be made ever more available. We must all look for means of reaching people before they choose suicide. Rarely is suicide a consciously, or even spiritually, fully navigated event. When it truly is, then the individual is making clear choices and is fully conscious of the impact of this event upon the self and others.

Various religions have various views on suicide and it is up to each Reader to choose her or his own approach to suicide. This book does not take a position on either suicide or euthanasia.

*This book does, however, advocate in favor of an adult individual's right to choose her or his own view on these matters — and right to decide how and when to be involved in the process of her or his own death.[23] Each person has the inalienable birthright right to choose for her or him self what sort of death to have, where, when, how, so long as that person is making a **responsible and fully informed choice, and not doing so in isolation**. The matter of responsible choice will be returned to later. **It may take a lifetime to prepare oneself to make a fully responsible and fully informed choice**.*

---

[23] It may be that the ability to leave the physical body at will without having to "commit suicide" is present within us. Numerous ancient cultures' teachings (as well as some modern day practices, some adapting ancient traditions, others being new models of this), continue to practice this form of self-willed, consciously selected BODY DEPARTURE. Steps describing this and other processes are presented in Volume 3 in this series, UNVEILING THE HIDDEN INSTINCT, and other steps in Volumes 4, 11, and 14 in this series, the HOW TO DIE AND SURVIVE books.

**CONSCIOUSLY MOVING THROUGH
LIFE'S CHANGES, TRANSITIONS, AND DEATHS**

SEEING BEYOND OUR LINE OF SIGHT

PART TWO

Fear Awareness-es
In Transition Processes

**CONSCIOUSLY MOVING THROUGH
LIFE'S CHANGES, TRANSITIONS, AND DEATHS**

6
Overcoming
The Apocalypse Syndrome

The reality of biological death is clear. Even healthy biological bodies can age and can die. Science may develop interventions that prolong biological life or someday further address biological death; however, science will continue to address the reality of biological death.

So, we feel that biological death looms out there, is in a sense, a fact of life. Biological death seems to stalk the living. At the same time, an expanded understanding of what death actually is or can be, seems to evade the living.

Unmasking Death

Now we are ready to unmask death and see its face. The mask itself is surprisingly easy to remove. Yet, behind the mask are many layers of faces, and many faces masking other faces. Close to the surface is the crust of that face, what we may feel to be acceptance, or perhaps surrender, or perhaps avoidance, and

also, of course, concern, worry, anxiety, trepidation ... these last sensations being various forms and levels of what we can call fear.

Distinguishing Between Fears

Fear is, of course, just a word. Fear is a so called "garbage pail" term for so many sensations and emotions all bundled into a general uneasy discomfort, and or anxiety, and or sometimes even foreboding. Yes, fear wears many faces, even many masks. Fear disguises itself as so many things.

Fear's disguise is frequently so effective that we do not realize that fear is present. Fear affects much of what goes on within and around us. So much fear is so very subconscious that we may even miss recognizing that it is present and affecting us, perhaps even at times driving us.

Let's examine this fear, look it in the eye. Have you ever been concerned, worried, anxious, fearful ... in some way? Was the fear clear to you, or more of a vague, free floating anxiety sort of sensation? Have you ever examined your own fear-like feelings? What sensations and emotions are behind or bundled into this fear? What sensations and emotions are masking this

fear? Did this fear ever disguise itself as something else? Did something else ever disguise itself as this fear? Was any of this fear a help or a hindrance to you?

To master in-life and seeming end-of-life transition, whatever the sort of death or transition being faced, we must see the difference between two basic types of fear, one a help and one a hindrance to survival.

When used well, fear serves a purpose. However, when used well, what we may sense to be or directly call "fear" is better described as *protective (and even proactive) awareness*. For example, feeling very anxious, even quite fearful, of something such as the possibility of an auto accident does less to prevent that something, such as that accident, than being very alert, highly aware of the other vehicles, people, animals on the road.

Paying attention is a very good idea. Being so scared that you cannot protect yourself is not a good idea. Being so hypervigilant that you are over responding to a concern or a fear is not being wisely vigilant. Blinding fear is not protective awareness. Blinding fear is a distraction from important information.

When fear clouds the consciousness, it is not being used well; it may be distracting or distorting, forming a *blinding fear*. Examining this fear to better understand it can help in navigating this fear itself, as well as the transitions this either vague or obvious fear may be affecting.

Sense Distinctions

Sensations such as anxiety, worry, various forms of low level and higher level subconscious and conscious fear, cloud the ***conscious management of the transition process***. Important attention and decision making, as well as other brain functions, can be interfered with by fear-like emotions. We must therefore understand forms of fear.

Many of the fears we experience we know we are experiencing, although we may not see in full the forms of fear these are or may be. Other of these fears we do not see affecting us. What these fears actually are may not be clear given that these may be running largely on subconscious and even collective unconscious levels.

Confusing These Fears

The distinction between the *blinding fear* and the *protective awareness* referred to earlier in this chapter is also especially critical on the population and societal levels. Not everyone who warns of physical, environmental, political, economic, or other danger or disaster is sick with blinding fear. Some of these persons are calling important developments to our attention, suggesting that, in order to have a conscious say in, or conscious response to, the course of events and developments, we can pay attention and maybe even take action.

Too often, those who seek to alert us to conditions, situations, events, or forces which may affect us undesirably and overtake us against our wills, are criticized or labeled as "paranoid" or "overly fearful" or "wrong" or even "crazy." Here, the protective awareness function is being incorrectly labeled as blinding fear.

This confusion over this reverse labelling is unfortunate, as protective awareness is frequently of great, even essential, value. We are frequently confused regarding the blinding-fear-driven and the protective-awareness-driven messages we hear. For

example, a respectable futurist may be taken far too lightly. Discerning the difference between a flat out fantasy and a sound warning is KEY.

flat out fantasy →→→ versus ←←← sound warning

But, do we have this discernment KEY in our possession? Knowing the difference is indeed a challenge.

We think of sirens as helpful, even essential, warning sounds coming from fire engines, police cars, air raid warnings, etc. We trust that these sirens are sounded to protect us in some way. However, do we carry within us a deep distrust of warnings, knowing that not all warnings are accurate or even protective?

Think of the story of the siren (found in ancient mythology) where the term "siren song" referred to an appeal or cry that was hard to resist, even seductive, but that if heeded would lead to a bad result.

Reading Our Messages

Messages, invitations, and even warnings can indeed be seductive. They can carry a momentum and magnetism of their own. Therefore, we must keep ourselves clear enough emotionally to discern the difference between a seductive false warning and a too often ignored valid one. Fear can muddle our ability to recognize the difference.

false warning → → → versus ← ← ← valid warning

Certainly, there is a problem knowing what to believe, how to tell the difference between useful information coming out of protective awareness, and the static and chaos that can come with the projection of blinding fear.

We Humans have lived with so many fear-inducing lies for so long that we confuse these with valid warnings of possible or actual, even impending, danger. It becomes frighteningly difficult to tell the difference.

**Could it be that
this disabling confusion
benefits control mechanisms
we have yet to recognize?**

We will return to this matter when we talk about the fears of death, and the various *mis- and dis- informations about death*, that may be generating these fears.

projection of blinding fear
→ versus ←
actual protective awareness

Why are we so frequently unable to clearly sense this difference between protective awareness and blinding fear? This is perhaps because we have been genetically, culturally, and spiritually programmed to carry within us a **masking condition** that interferes with our *clear discernment of protective information.*

What masks our awareness may be generally unrecognized while being labeled as an emotion such as free floating anxiety or as other conditions such as depression.

When Fear Is Neither Protective Nor Productive

Entire populations have been controlled by manipulating their fear functions. Some fear is falsely generated. Other fear is based on actual conditions and even threats to safety. I call both of these *fear generators*.

Responses to fear can be impulsive, deeply driven instinctive fight, flight, freeze responses that are frequently

essential life saving and life protecting responses. Yet, these responses can also run awry. This is when the fear response with its fight flight freeze impulses can be not only incorrect, but even unproductive and even dangerous.

When Apocalypse Is On Our Minds

I have worked with many persons experiencing what I have come to define as the *apocalypse syndrome*. The *apocalypse syndrome* afflicts many who feel a sort of impending doom, yes, with various elements of fear, anxiety, depression, yet also relating to what may be vaguely accurate sensations that life is in peril now or in the future.

For several decades now, a certain percentage of persons coming in to see me have been talking about serious concerns they have that Human life (perhaps all life) on Earth is in danger. Some find themselves almost immobilized with this condition. Others find themselves making what they feel may even be unwise decisions driven by this condition.

This *apocalypse syndrome* can cloud the discernment process, and can make it difficult to know whether a fear is one we must listen to for our own and others' safety, or a free floating

sensation bundling fear, anxiety, and other emotional states. Now, what can take place is that these emotions attach themselves to the nearest possible or even impossible problem or threat. Now, transition navigation can become muddled, confused, impaired.

Confusion and fear mix together into a blurry cocktail of unknowns, which tends to at least emotionally disempower or paralyze those who drink it. Now the *conscious management* of in-life and seeming end-of-life transition is clouded, less aware in its *transition navigation* process.

See This Apocalypse Syndrome

This condition, this *apocalypse syndrome*, is riddled with real plus imagined sensations, and or questions about these, which can confuse the mind:

What is the difference between a real and an imagined sensation, a real or an imagined fear? Does it matter whether a sensation is reality-based or not? After all, what is reality? What is a valid concern and what is not? How do we know?

If kept to a dull roar, and considered calmly, these can be very good questions. Using these questions as part of a process of learning to *discern for oneself* what the choices are, what beliefs can be accepted or discarded, is part of the awakening of the mind, the spirit, the self, the *conscious* metacognition[24]—*the aware consciousness*. Coming up with personal ways of knowing what is true for oneself, without outside influence dictating this, is KEY.

Apocalypse Teachings

Fear, whether masking itself as something else, hiding itself, or quite obvious, is such a driver.

Take some time to think about the meaning of the word, "apocalypse," and what your conscious mind does with this concept. Whether or not your subconscious mind pays any attention to this concept is less important for the moment.

---

[24] See the in depth definition and development of the *conscious awareness concept* offered in other books in this KEYS TO CONSCIOUSNESS AND SURVIVAL SERIES, such as UNVEILING THE HIDDEN INSTINCT.

The term "apocalypse" comes from the Greek word "apokalypsis," or "disclosure." Apocalypse was originally defined as some kind of major all-involving disaster in which forces of good and evil would clash, and from which, in the end, only supernatural intervention could preserve good.

According to most traditional definitions of apocalypse, communication with divine forces would disclose or reveal the timing, the force, and the characteristics of an apocalypse. Many religions therefore include "divine revelation." Some of these revelations are said to come to Humans directly from a god. However, apparently in said reality, only a few Humans can read these messages. Many other revelations are said to come from a god, but through designated go-betweens or intermediaries who may be shamans, religious leaders, or persons with special abilities or special statuses.

Most major religions include references to one or more apocalypses or cataclysms. These are oft said to take place at the end of a cycle of time. At the end of such a cycle: piety is said to be dead; fire, drought, and famine to ravage the Earth; a century or a long spell of death to follow. According to several apocalypse stories, despite flooding, all the moisture on and in the Earth will begin to dry up. Eventually, a universal conflagration of some sort will eliminate the last of the Human occupants and all the Earth will be consumed in a vast whirlpool of flame. There is usually said to be a supernatural or higher power-determined way for "believers" and "the chosen ones" to survive.

This is common *apocalypse teaching* carried by many of the world's religions, and also most likely deep within our cellular and or genetic memories. Depictions of this process do appear again and again in Human religion and mythology. Many of these myths include the same ingredients--increasing tribulation; the moral dissolution of Human kind; the emergence of some kind of major war; the fracturing and collapse of the Earth's crust; and, later, the sinking of land masses, even entire continents, into the sea; the atmosphere becoming darkened; stars (including comets and meteors and maybe even moons) crashing down to Earth from the sky; and a massive fire of some sort filling much of the Earth's atmosphere.

Of course, this end is also a beginning, as new yugas or time cycles begin after major apocalypses, with the same cycles repeatedly appearing. Eventually, the same ultimate fate evolves. Again and again, from the spoils, from ashes of the cosmic fire, arises the phoenix, the flight of life, born anew. Even this ultimate ending is a beginning, a transition to a new state.

Not To Minimize Apocalypse

This quick overview is not to minimize the reality of apocalypse. Modern science tells us that the Earth has surely witnessed comet impacts and massive disasters of global proportions which killed off entire groups of species--dinosaurs, for example. And such disasters can happen again; they may be part of our larger cosmic destiny.

There is more to history on Earth than we teach ourselves. Much of the truth about Earth's history has been lost. However, the collective memory has managed to keep some form of this information alive for us all, preserving it not only in mythical and religious form throughout history, but also in symbolic imagery deeply embedded in the collective memory or mind--

perhaps even encoded into the genetics which grow that mind/brain.

Are We Coded With This
Apocalypse Syndrome

Here, we must pause to wonder how, if images of apocalypse are indeed coded into our collective memories, *how* did those images get there, and are they placed there to protect us or to scare us into being more easily controlled?

Are these images manipulated by those who understand the power to be had in using people's, even whole populations', fears and fear mechanisms to control them?

What sort of mechanism could have been generated or implanted into us with sensations of possible doom, cataclysm — with *blinding fear* serving as blocker of *protective awareness*? Is the *apocalypse syndrome* deeply buried within our programming? If so, what form of evolution or design would have generated this dangerous function within our species?

Certainly, one answer here is that even the essential and protective, and at times even life-saving, fight-flight-freeze

impulse can run awry. This answer implies that this necessary protective awareness function itself malfunctions, sometimes.

However, there are other possible explanations such as: Perhaps we are coded not to fully protect ourselves from ineffective, dangerous, blinding fear. If so, the *apocalypse syndrome* may be quite deeply buried within our programming. What a way to hold us captive, to weaken our awareness functions at times we may most need these.

What a way to have us held in a *not-seeing state*. This is a *not-accessing state* of *programmed-in lessened awareness* that we are experiencing now -- at a time when we most need our own rightful access to our continuum of consciousness to survive. It is indeed time for us to wake up.

7
Personal Apocalypse

Whatever its means of and motive for coming to us may be, information about the possibility of global or massive disaster is useful. On a very deep level, Humankind desires this knowledge. This knowledge may allow for heightened survival awareness and fine-tuned survival oriented behaviors.

Spillover Sensation

Humankind does not want to be kept in the dark. Humanity therefore instinctively keeps its sensors out-- maintains a protective awareness regarding past, present, and potential future issues, dangers, even cataclysms.

The problem is that with this healthy instinct comes a deeply buried blindness. Even if various people do not feel themselves to be fearful, they cannot help but be affected by imagery buried deep within the collective mind.

A spillover sensation, a residual sense, even a deep underlying sensation of fear, persists and is carried in images,

traces of memory. These traditionally and genetically preserved sensations can bring on the great Fear of Death. This great fear itself can cloud *conscious navigation of transition and thus conscious survival-oriented behaviors.*

This discussion is important in that it traces the source of our individual awareness of possible disaster back through Human history and Earth history to pictures of actual disaster that have indeed taken place and can indeed happen again.

Protective Awareness

Every living thing has deeply ingrained survival mechanisms that should promote an ongoing protective awareness in each of us. Yet, we sometimes translate this high and pure awareness down into lower emotional states that frequently cloud the *intelligently protective awareness.* Fear (and various emotions bundled into the fear package) may take the form of lower emotional states clouding our protective awareness, clouding our *conscious management of our awareness-es and transition experiences.*

Many people bring awareness and acceptance of the reality of global, solar, galactic, even cosmic, cataclysm down to the

personal level. As a result of this natural instinctive translation, they start seeing potential apocalypse everywhere. Protective awareness and blinding fear are then mingled. Perceptions are then clouded and very subjective.

This is how personal apocalypses, real or imagined, are tailor-made for us, by our subjective perceptions of our experiences and of the information we have regarding possible upcoming experiences. These personalized apocalypses can include and confuse real and imagined, global and local, population and personal, major and minor, traumatic life experiences, transitions: changes, endings, deaths.

And, to further cloud the issue, as problematic as this confusion can be, it contains within it some degree of honesty: a child screaming in pain on the other side of the planet is felt on some level by a sensitive person standing here. Just knowing this suffering is taking place somewhere – no matter how we come to know this – allows us awareness of suffering.

Yes, on some level, all of us are always in touch with the sensations being experienced by members of our own species, wherever they are, and likely even by other life forms

everywhere.²⁵ (Some nursing mothers report they have discovered this sensitivity when their babies cry across town, out of earshot, and these mothers nevertheless respond.) We are all likely this sensitive, whether or not we recognize this.

This is a basic survival mechanism -- sensitivity to the needs and condition of the species. *Personal apocalypse consciousness* is a reality, whether or not a person is conscious of having it. Population pain IS personal suffering -- even when this translation is entirely subconscious. Yes, we share pain, just as we share positive experiences.²⁶

Positive Apocalypse Consciousness

KEY forms of apocalypse awareness are with and within us. It would be dishonest to say that intense experiences, challenging transitions, events which may be perceived as terrible, will never

---

²⁵ See detailed development of this *conscious awareness* concept in other books in this KEYS TO CONSCIOUSNESS AND SURVIVAL SERIES such as Volumes 5 and 6, OVERRIDING THE EXTINCTION SCENARIO, Parts One and Two, and also Volume 3, UNVEILING THE HIDDEN INSTINCT, and also Volumes 4, 11, and 14, the HOW TO DIE AND SURVIVE books.

²⁶ See discussion of links among personal and population perceptions in UNVEILING THE HIDDEN INSTINCT.

take place. But it is also dishonest to say that there is no productive way of consciously perceiving these.

Positive apocalypse consciousness is essential. This constructive view and use of our *instinctive apocalypse awareness* will purify the application of *protective awareness* and reduce its being mingled with blinding fear. Positive apocalypse consciousness is a state of knowing how to admit to oneself the difference between blinding fear and protective awareness, and how to resist labeling one's sensations as one or the other of these fears -- when others (often inaccurately) may label these for you.

Meeting The Challenge

Positive apocalypse consciousness involves a sense of rising to meet the challenge of any transition, of any in-life and seeming end-of-life death. Seeing a purpose, a positive outcome, as a distinct possibility -- even if that positive outcome is simply that one CAN consciously move through a passage, a transition, even an ordeal -- is essential.

Allow the ideas offered here to dialogue with your own heart, mind, and soul. Try these ideas on, test these ideas in daily life. Question as much of this as you feel driven to. Honest questioning and ongoing dialogue is a means of discovering truth for yourself and for all of us. And this is the surest route to knowledge–your knowledge, and our knowledge, our species knowledge, our living knowledge.

Fear, if read with understanding, is a signal. We must learn to read our own and others' fears for their meaning. We must learn to prevent fear from blocking us, disturbing us, withholding from us our deeply ingrained true abilities to *navigate change and transition to a new place, a higher state well* BEYOND OUR LINE OF SIGHT.

PART THREE

Physical Death
As Transition

**CONSCIOUSLY MOVING THROUGH
LIFE'S CHANGES, TRANSITIONS, AND DEATHS**

8
Looking To The Frontier: Seeing and Extending Beyond Physical Death

This chapter discusses physical death: <u>first</u>, to take some of the mystery out of it; <u>second</u>, to realize that physical death can be a valuable metaphor for all forms of change and transition; <u>third</u>, to begin to see death as not an ending, rather as an ongoing transition; and <u>fourth</u>, to begin to suggest that there may be the option of *moving on as a personal consciousness* from the physical death transition, as the chapters following this one discuss.

The possibility, and reality, of physical death is for many the greatest subject of concern, perhaps even of anxiety, even of fear. Of all shifts and changes we may face, the *perceived permanency* of physical death makes it all the more difficult to think about. *Yet, it is the fearful perception of the death process rather than death itself that may be feared.*

Death is so very misunderstood. And how can we live when we do not understand death, such a major part of life?

This book also asks: can we change how we live as we: (1) ever more consciously approach and navigate in-life and seeming end-of-life death; and as we (2) manage our transitions with the goal of extending our *continuum of consciousness* beyond physical death, beyond our present LINE OF SIGHT?

Physical Death

Let's talk about what many consider the "real" thing: physical death. No use waiting until we are dying to prepare. Let's start now.

Given that we accept physical death as one more transition in the ongoing cycle of life, perhaps one of the most if not the most profound, why not prepare for it all our lives? Why reach a physical death without having prepared for it all along?

This is not morbid, nor a troubled fascination with death, rather this is a healthy, realistic, and elevated approach to an event that we all face, and for which all of life's other transitions can prepare us. In fact, the way we live, the way we master the transitions we undergo in our lives, will maximize the roles we can play in our transitions *out* of our own physical bodies.

Death Is A Metaphor

No discussion of endings, transitions, as being small and large deaths, in-life and seeming end-of-life deaths, can go on without some review of the stages of actual physical death. This is not only because physical death is what is most commonly thought of when the word "death" is used, and not only because physical death is a profound process we generally call "death." This is also because physical death is a powerful *metaphor* for many other endings, transitions.

You will see the value of this comparison between physical death and other forms of transition as you read on. Try not to allow a fear of death, or the sense that "this has nothing to do with my life right now," to stop you from stepping deeply into this chapter. Or return to these chapters (8, 9, and 10) on physical death later, when you feel yourself ready.

Do read these chapters in the order you prefer. It is safe to wander here. All your transitions, especially the more difficult ones, are parallel or even in some ways similar to physical death transitions. See what parallels and similarities you find . . . .

Conscious Dying Is Your Right

Each and every physical death is different. However, there are general similarities among these. Some of the variation in the dying process relates to the style of death one chooses, (if one has or takes the opportunity to choose, that is).

Now, contrary to what most of us have been taught, there are choices in death. As suggested in earlier chapters, this statement is not to balk at the rules society has constructed regarding suicide and euthanasia. Again, Readers' differing views regarding suicide and euthanasia are their own and are not contested here. Instead, another concept is being set forth:

You have the choice to **educate your consciousness** *about dying. In fact,* **conscious dying** *is your right.* It is important to know whether you might be able, and if so how, to stay connected to your consciousness while you die, whether or not you are deemed medically conscious at the time.

This book suggests that we may have the option of developing ourselves to be ever more conscious during our transition processes, to allow ourselves to stay connected to our consciousnesses, to our *selves*.

Get To Know Consciousness

Let's be clear about consciousness here. Being conscious by medical definition may not be the only way of being conscious. It may be that there is an ongoing consciousness no matter whether the person is medically conscious or in a coma or in another state.

In fact, even in a "waking" so-called by medical terms "fully conscious" state, there are overlaps between levels of consciousness. And, even in a waking state, we may think we are more conscious than we are (or less conscious than we are!!!). Let's just assume that there are, or may be, *degrees of consciousness,* even degrees, in medical terms, of "unconscious" states.

There may indeed be *degrees* of consciousness, not only in waking life, but also during the dying process itself. Adding to this range of our degrees of consciousness, this book discusses the possibility that:

> **we may have the option to
> develop ourselves in ways that can
> extend our degrees of consciousness into the time
> after our apparent physical death has taken place.**

We may have the option to further develop our awareness, our aware consciousness, to extend our *continuum of consciousness* BEYOND our present physical plane, biological body's, LINE OF SIGHT. (See later chapters in this book, where this *continuum of consciousness* is defined.)

How do these degrees of consciousness appear to us?

On Biologically Based Consciousness

First, let's talk about biologically-based consciousness. If perhaps some degree of biologically-based consciousness lives in each and every cell of the physical biological body, then the aspect of the consciousness which is biologically-based may not die all at the same time. Whether or not it is agreed that this is the case, it is likely that the physical body does not die all at once.

In fact, modern science is discovering that many a body appears dead and is pronounced dead while what may be billions, even trillions, of its cells are still alive. Some medical theories actually propose an immediate lowering of the nearly dead and even already pronounced dead body temperature to just above freezing, inducing a sort of hypothermia, to allow the cells to reoxygenate, to refurbish, themselves. This has been suggested as a possible revival of life after the body has been deemed dead.

On Blurring The Boundary

While modern medicine continues to blur its own line between physical life and death, philosophical, theological, and spiritual studies of the mind and soul have long done, and continue to do, the same thing in very different ways.

We really have no way to fully prove by physical plane scientific terms that the consciousness dies. A heart beat and a brain wave may not be sufficient means of proof here. We cannot prove there is nothing beyond the physical by using only physical (including medical) measures to do this.

Think of the old story about the sail boat heading for the horizon. You are on the shore watching. The boat appears smaller and smaller as it moves away from you. Eventually, you can no longer see that sail boat, it has crossed the horizon.

This does not mean that sail boat has disappeared out of all existence. All this means is that you cannot see -- with your eyes

-- the sail boat. You cannot say the sail boat has sailed out of existence. You can only say the sailboat has sailed out of your present LINE OF SIGHT.

Now, imagine that your dying friend is moving away from you, dying as we call it. This friend is leaving the physical body, crossing over – crossing the horizon line between the physical reality and the reality beyond. This person's biologically-based consciousness moves away from you something like the sail boat.

But, this does not mean that the person's personal consciousness is entirely out of existence. You cannot know this by looking at the body that this person's personal consciousness was once tied to. You cannot see the answer with your physical eyes (eyes which were developed to see in this physical dimension). There is no proof that the "dying" person's consciousness is anything but past what you see (from where you stand) as being the horizon.

SEEING BEYOND OUR LINE OF SIGHT may reveal more to us, or at least allow for the discovery of more, or the development of more.

On Crossing The Boundary

So the consciousness may *cross over*. This concept suggests that the consciousness can perhaps remain in existence even if you do not see it so doing. This book suggests that we have, or can consciously develop, the option and the capability of so doing. The consciousness may be able to develop the option of crossing over -- alive, well, still intact, conscious.[27]

All the more reason to instill as much consciousness as possible into one's understanding of in-life and seeming end-of-life transition processes--and in fact to prepare for the possibility of *ever more conscious crossing over*, **transitioning, what some say is dying.**

And all the more reason to understand that perhaps conscious dying can take place whether or not a person is medically defined as being in a state of consciousness, or is said to be semi-consciousness, or unconsciousness. Medically defined

---

[27] As I explain in other books in this KEYS TO CONSCIOUSNESS AND SURVIVAL SERIES, such as Volumes 5 and 6, the OVERRIDING THE EXTINCTION SCENARIO books, we are in the process of evolving, and can choose to further evolve the non-physical aspects of ourselves.

consciousness is focused on biologically-based consciousness.[28] Here in this book, we are focusing on something else, on the option the consciousness may have to reach beyond this, the opportunity the consciousness may have to develop *the capability to consciously cross over, even eventually independent of biology.*

Here is the possibility of the ***handing of the reigns over to the non-biological consciousness***. We might want to think in terms of the *transfer* of control: the physical body houses, or perhaps borrows, the consciousness for a while (during the physical lifetime) and then returns it to its non-physical home. Or perhaps the consciousness always lived there, beyond the physical realm ... along its own *continuum of consciousness.*

For Those Who Question, Call This Metaphor

About now, if not earlier in the reading of this book, there will be Readers who question this thinking. This is perfectly acceptable. In fact, this is most desirable. All that is presented here comes in the form of ideas to be tried on, thought about, traveled around with and within. Questioning is good. In fact,

---

[28] See the discussion of biological versus non-biological bases of consciousness in the book, UNVEILING THE HIDDEN INSTINCT.

questioning may allow an inquisitive mind to take all this in in the form of metaphor. Thinking, having ideas, generates corresponding events in the brain, opening existing and new pathways for messages to travel, and sites for new information to perhaps be processed in new ways.

Metaphor is a wonderful teaching tool. In this case, we want to be able to apply the metaphor of physical death to all changes, endings, transitions, we are experiencing in what we call *life*.

We also can take what we learn from living through in-life transitions to our appreciation of the physical death process itself. *Metaphor is a powerful vehicle for the transmission of this knowledge.* Imagination is triggered when we put our minds to work on metaphors.

Imagination has opened many doors. So, where indecision regarding what may be happening exists, simply explore various possibilities via the imagination. Call all this science fiction if this allows for the consideration of the possibilities presented here and in the other volumes in this series.

Open The Frontier:
Find Life Along The Continuum

Of course, imagination itself does not produce fact. However, imagination allows the mind and brain to explore possibilities, to open doors of awareness. You can begin to communicate with your mind and brain, even with your awareness and its consciousness. You can begin to talk to your conscious metacognition. You can do all this as you develop the range of your *continuum of awareness* and thus of your *continuum of consciousness*.

Let's say we have, or can choose to have, **non-physical (or beyond physical) territory** for ourselves. Let's say we can consciously extend our **continuum of consciousness** while here in this physical plane living in our physical bodies. We can generate possibilities, link brain cells and ideas, open doors in our minds, create learnings, envision worlds beyond those we are presently finding ourselves in every day.

We can be building, constructing, new regions, new domains, opening new territory for ourselves. **Welcome to life along the continuum of consciousness, where we can see well beyond OUR present LINE OF SIGHT.**

9
Steps And Phases Of Death Transition

While they do not necessarily correspond, several different phases of death have been described by members of the medical, the philosophical, the literary, and the spiritual fields. Reducing these down for simplicity's sake here, we can say that: (a) there are at least three phases or stages of death (although, as noted earlier, physical death has increasingly hazy boundaries); and then that, (b) there may be phases past what is recognized as physical death.

In Terms Of Phases Of Dying

We can think of these phases in terms of the death of the physical body and its biologically-based consciousness by degrees (from a more medical perspective). Or, we can think of these phases in terms of the death of the physical body -- and then: *the transition into a different form of the less physical components of the self and its consciousness.* (This thinking tends to appear in more esoteric and or spiritual terms, although

there may at times be overlaps between medical and esoteric and spiritual explanations of these phases).

Merging these and expanding upon the merging of the medical and the spiritual phases of death, we arrive at an interesting place – we can see death both ways at the same time.

Note that the dying process does not necessarily begin when an individual is given a certain amount of time to live, or when an individual contracts a "fatal" disease or injury.

Medical doctors do not necessarily see their "dying" patients as "dying" the very moment they begin dying. We might say that the death process is ongoing and in many cases, perhaps most cases, undetected for a very long time. We do not know when most dying processes begin. We may recast dying as transitioning, and then see ourselves as always in transition.

Are We Always Living And Dying

From some perspectives, physical death begins when we stop growing, when we become adults. This would mean that we spend most of our adult lives dying. Every day we do live, yes, but every day we also maybe die a bit. We can also most

definitely say that we spend every moment of our lives living, that every moment we do live a bit, or a lot for that matter. Living and dying mesh and are perhaps not best described as separate processes with specific frames and endings. Again, transition is a more inclusive definition.

**CONSCIOUSLY MOVING THROUGH
LIFE'S CHANGES, TRANSITIONS, AND DEATHS**

10
A First Phase Of Death

Generally speaking, medicine will tell us that we actually begin the formal *dying process* itself when the body begins to physically shut down, little by little quitting its physical activities. Up until that point, we are told, formal dying has not actually started.

Supporting The Life Of The Physical

Some say that when life support is administered to save a life, this is an interruption of the dying process to save that life. However, interrupting the dying process is resuming, hopefully, the living process. Life is so valuable, it makes complete sense we do everything we can to save a life, including keep the person alive while working to provide medical care that will prolong that life or heal that person (or patient as that person is likely being called at this time).

Of course, not all administerings of life support are to save the lives of dying people. Sometimes, life support extends a life, sometimes it eases suffering, sometimes it helps family members who wish to have done everything they can for a dying loved one feel that they have.

Motivations for the use of life support come in many forms and are frequently mixed. It is a good idea for each of us to give serious thought to what we want done for and to us while we are undergoing various phases of transition or death, and to make this clear to our doctors and loved ones well in advance.

[This book seeks to add another dimension to the concept of "life support." Where of course, all that can be done to save a life must be done, we of course focus quite logically on life support for those in need while still in their physical bodies. The question is, might we eventually understand that persons who have left their physical bodies may also benefit from some form of support, what I have described elsewhere as AFTER LIFE SUPPORT. (See Chapters 11, 12,13, 14.)]

Experience Of First Stage Varies

Quite often, (although not always), the first stage of actual physical dying is said to be experienced *semi-consciously*. Where it is not, the dying person can nevertheless be more conscious than he or she may appear to be to medical personnel or other

onlookers. Some piece of the mind, the self, the awareness, the conscious awareness, may be present. (See the chapters on out-of-body and near-death experiences in Volume 3, UNVEILING THE HIDDEN INSTINCT.)

Usually, early in the dying process, blood pressure substantially reduces. The brain therefore finds itself running short of its normal supply of oxygen and sugar. So the brain turns on a compensatory mechanism which dilates its blood vessels and draws extra blood from wherever it might be stored in the body. What this does is give the sugar-hungry brain a brief increase in its blood sugar. The brain hangs on to its biologically-fueled inner consciousness this way.

At this point, the brain is, for a brief time, receiving a much enriched supply of food. With this increase in brain food, the dying person is able to flashback on, or even to rapidly review, his or her entire life. Some form of what is likely still biologically-based consciousness is actually intensified here, although little emotion is felt in these flashback moments. This is because this intense review is a higher cognitive activity, likely a mental body activity, with little if any involvement of lower emotional processes.

Is there already a *cross over sensation* present at this time? Is the SELF, the awareness, already "walking in two worlds" so to speak, being both a physical being and a being not tied to biology? This notion of crossing over is an issue discussed further in the following chapters.

Brain Working At Feverous Pitch

At this time, the brain, mainly the cortex, is working at a feverous pitch. Now, it is consuming sugar faster than it can get it. This results in the brain's sensing that it cannot continue to fuel the intense flashback process. When this awareness is registered, the brain begins moving into the second stage of physical dying. The brain can be operating at a very high frequency now, maintaining what are called rapid rhythmical beta waves with some spurts of alpha. This can generate what some Human meditators can bring about for themselves without physically dying -- a sense of bliss, a transcendent sense.

Whether or not appearing to be conscious in medical terms, the brain may be conscious of being in this euphoria-like state.

Yet, this is not really an emotional experience in the way we experience joy in daily life. This is a very special, very high, state somewhat like a non-emotional bliss.

This stage of physical dying draws to a close. Up to this time, medical or other efforts to revive the dying person, to return the dying person to the mortal body, can still be successful. Many a dying individual, persuaded by the profound euphoria, is committed to dying by now. Now, many a physically dying person "feels" he or she "wants" to die this physical death.

Remember

Remember that, when you find yourself in this state, you do have a right to move on. You can choose the timing and nature of this step for yourself, if you have taught yourself to know this. And, in reality, we all know this already. We just need to remember now to *activate the awareness* that may be carried deep within us .

Given that there has been a long social training not to know this, not to know how to die at will without committing suicide, we may need assistance remembering. It is therefore best to

begin remembering before encountering physical death, to give ourselves little trainings about, and notes for, the future – and to do this in the now.

Every (even daily-life) transition process offers practice in ever more consciously moving from one phase to the next (and also from one stage within a phase to the next stage within that phase).

As you live, always know that every transition offers practice in transition itself, thus practice in extending OUR LINE OF SIGHT.

We can allow our consciousness to sensitize to, to see, the parallels. We can practice, even master, these living transitions and eventually even physical death processes, perhaps even after life processes.[29]

At this point in your dying, it is going to be important to remember that you may still be able to make a "conscious" decision to either go ahead and biologically die, or to come back

---

[29] Exercises and understandings for ever more consciously moving through these transitions are offered in Volumes 4, 11, and 14 in this series, the HOW TO DIE AND SURVIVE books.

into your biological body. You may actually find you can make this decision without medical intervention pushing you in either direction. You are actually quite powerful at this juncture. You just need to know this at this time. You are rarely told this, even though this knowledge is your birthright.

If the dying person moves on into what is called in medical speak, "death," the next stage of physical dying begins here. Now the body will stop breathing, the physical eyes will stop seeing, although they have most likely stopped looking before this time. The brain will stop running, being out of sugar. The dying individual may be aware of these sensations, yet in a detached, unemotional, and neutral way.

**CONSCIOUSLY MOVING THROUGH
LIFE'S CHANGES, TRANSITIONS, AND DEATHS**

11
Cross Over Sensation

The concept, *afterlife support*, was suggested in the previous chapter.

We can see the possibilities for assisting ourselves and others move through the phases of death, *crossing over* from a physical, biologically based existence to a new place along the *continuum of consciousness*.

Crossing Over

The previous chapter closes at the seeming end of life, or as we might say here, at the *seeming* end of *biological* life. The last words, if any, will have been uttered -- usually mumbled or whispered -- by now.

One of the last physical sensations may be the sensation, again not unpleasant, that the mouth is filled with the sense of thickness, something like a non-physical cement. While this is actually a physical sensation, this is also likely far more than a physical sensation.

This may be a *parallel sensation*, one we cannot precisely measure in terms of our current scientific tools. We may want to note that such a sensory experience may exist outside the range of our normal physical sensory mechanisms (such as taste, touch, sight, smell, hearing).

How we carry sensation into our non-physical existence is a complex matter discussed in other books in this KEYS TO CONSCIOUSNESS AND SURVIVAL SERIES. Where we sense something when out of our physical bodies, we may be:

(a) still tied to our physicality; and or …

(b) still remembering sensory functions of physicality; and or …

(c) interpreting what we are aware of in terms of previously known forms of sensory experience, and or …

(d) forming new sensory, or better stated *perceptive mechanisms*, that work for us when we are becoming non-physical.

Here again is the matter of crossing over. Can we maintain our awareness, our aware consciousness, in this cross over

process? Yes, with the knowledge that this is our option, we can.[30]

Crossing Over May Be
A Complex Yet Simple Transition

The sense of the mouth filling with a thickness or cement-like effect has been reported by many persons who have experienced being close to death. This sensation may be about as tangible as anything non-physical may be.

Here, in this time of crossing over, is where the *cross over sensation,* or *cross over transition,* may be experienced just about as tangibly as anything this non-physical or ethereal can be. Here is where the sensation or impression of cement filling the mouth can be viewed as being the cement of the ether flowing in, of the non-physical reality flowing in.

This is a complex sensation in that the feeling of cement does suggest something thick and heavy, something very physical. But, what is perceived as heavy is the physicality that

---

[30] Indeed, presenting and developing this option is KEY in the material presented in this KEYS TO CONSCIOUSNESS AND SURVIVAL SERIES of books, ebooks, audiobooks, processes, and workshops.

is being left behind. The sensation of cement filling the mouth, or of physicality being left behind, is thus full of information such as:

> One: We now have the awareness of something we have been feeling all along, throughout our physical lives, the awareness of being physical, and being therefore weighed down with physicality. Separating from physicality gives us, perhaps more clearly than ever, awareness of the tremendous thickness and weight which physicality – even the slightest bit of even skeletal physicality – gives us to carry.
>
> Two: The cement-like sensation is also the coming of a numbness to the tactile and sensory functions as these have been known in the physical body. Some of the last sensation is the sensation of no feeling, numbness, a bit like the anesthetic felt at the dentist's office. And the mouth, being close to the physical brain, may still have enough fuel to sense the physical numbing.
>
> Three: And, what makes all of this yet more complex and wondrous is that ... the conceptual or actual contact with

the non-physical dimension, the *"ether"* as it is oft called, is likely being made. While this other non-physical dimension of reality is always present and available to us, we are not necessarily alert to its presence. Even when we are alert to its presence, the billions of micro-mini sensations coming to us at all times when we are in a physical body tend to drown out the ongoing flood of pure etheric essences which we may always be touch with – swimming in -- without realizing we are.

Now, in this cross over phase of death, physical sensations retreat, diminish, then fade away, and in flows the magnificent non-physical reality. Be ready for this rush of awareness, as this brings so much that seems to be new to us. We are now able to be aware with new eyes so to speak, non-physical eyes. Before this moment, we may have barely begun to define non-physicality, to know what is there for us -- as before now, we were largely restricted to concepts and words formed by our physical -plane based biological brain.

Crossing over into non-physical reality has many characteristics. (Several books in this KEYS TO

CONSCIOUSNESS AND SURVIVAL SERIES delve further into these characteristics.) Here, let's simply say that this *crossing* can be as conscious as possible, and can be a many splendored *conscious transition experience*. (Note: whether or not we are medically defined as being physically conscious, we may be consciously experiencing this crossing over.)

Learning about this crossing over experience in advance is a wonderful way to train the consciousness to watch for these steps, and to travel these transitional steps adeptly, consciously.

Oh Look, I'm Still Here

The ether is not material in the sense of the three dimensional physical plane reality the physically dying person is leaving. The ether is more airy, if air can be something non-material for the purposes of this discussion. The ether is the realm (or dimension) into which the dying person may now be moving. Preparing in advance to enter this realm aware, and then to consciously navigate this realm, can be KEY.

And of course, the phrase, *enter this realm*, is more about *becoming aware of this realm*, as this realm is already here, we are already in this realm. This is indeed about an entry of our

awareness into this realm, or an extension of our awareness *to* this realm, as we are already existing along our *continuum of consciousness.*

Once this **transit** is completed, once this transit of our awareness, of our aware consciousness, is completed, we have *EXPANDED* OUR LINE OF SIGHT. Even during this transit (without medical or other intervention calling the individual part or all the way back), there will be no further physical sensation unless the dying individual chooses and believes, or imagines, there to be.

Imagines? Well, yes, imagining here is tricky. Imagination stretches the awareness, allows the awareness to investigate. (See other books in this KEYS TO CONSCIOUSNESS AND SURVIVAL SERIES where *the essential imagination function* is defined.) This imagination can not arise from the shut down physical brain at this point. Most persons who are able to be somewhat conscious during this time will sense, feel, imagine, that they are not in their physical bodies.

(Remember that this is a good time to observe how much of your sensation of reality you can conduct with your

consciousness, whether or not you have a functioning biological body or working biological sensory organs.)

Continuing Of Awareness

Now there can be a continued awareness of self, and at the same time, a looking "down" at the biological body which is being shed. Now it is more clear that the SELF is not being shed, that only the biological body is being shed. Some beings see someone kissing their physical bodies and experience a detached longing for a physical body again. Others, most others, may be rather relieved, even profoundly relieved, to let go. There is a *lighten*-ing sense, an *unweighten*-ing.

Remember to stay conscious here. You *can* stay conscious here. Knowing this is doing this and being this.

Practice in daily life, and notice when your "mind" is seeing, feeling, "thinking." Begin now to be in ever more conscious contact with what may become more and more experienced as the non-physical dimensions of yourself, of your mind, of your consciousness. This is who you are. Get to know better and better who survives: yes, you. Allow the undefined

aspects of you, of your non-physical self, to exist as ideas, images, sensations, within your mind and consciousness.

Observe yourself being consciously aware. Get to know your awareness, your aware consciousness. Talk to it, dance with it. Learn to stop regularly and take the time to notice: (a) *your location* in what you have been calling space and time; (b) even your *location* in your physical, emotional, and mental bodies; (c) even your ***location along your own continuum of consciousness.***

You are mapping your reality, your higher reality.

And, you are training your consciousness, your non-physical metacognition, to map its reality.[31] You are getting to know and to further define, further extend, your own personal *continuum of consciousness.*

Remember, this is your domain,
yours to know, to define,
to explore, to extend.

---

[31] Discussion of such mapping is continued in depth in other books in this KEYS TO CONSCIOUSNESS AND SURVIVAL SERIES such as NAVIGATING LIFE'S STUFF: DYNAMICS OF PERSONAL CHANGE, BOOK ONE, and also in HOW TO DIE AND SURVIVE, BOOK ONE.

Freeing The Soul

Letting go of physicality is critical here. You can remember that you can stay conscious as you do so. This is a KEY remembrance.

Also note again that staying conscious is not simply restricted to medical definitions of being conscious. Many a near death experience "survivor" has reported the experience of being conscious while deemed asleep or even medically unconscious.

The notion that we can understand and even train ourselves to stay with ourselves, with our consciousness, is essential in SEEING BEYOND OUR present and biological LINE OF SIGHT. We can indeed SEE and live BEYOND the seeming limits our experience of being in this physical plane has set for us.[32]

---

[32] Exercises for practicing holding onto consciousness in traveling the transition and even death processes are offered in Volume 3, UNVEILING THE HIDDEN INSTINCT, and then further exercises are offered in Volume 4, HOW TO DIE AND SURVIVE.

SEEING BEYOND OUR LINE OF SIGHT

It is important to understand the letting go or severance process. Physical death is the withdrawal of the soul or spirit or self, of the consciousness, from its primary biological anchors: the heart and the pineal gland in the brain.

This withdrawal from the heart and from the head cuts off the two streams of energy which are said to unite the ethereal soul with the physical body -- the blood stream and the endocrine stream or system. This cutting off severs the connection between physical body and non-physical body or bodies.

Sometimes a physical, biological (and even an emotional) body resists the departure of the personal consciousness that has inhabited it. Then this severance process may feel slower and perhaps a little more entangled. It might be better said that some beings, perhaps not understanding this process, do not fully cut or release their own ties, their cords. These are in essence energetic strings which may perhaps, at least to some extent, be pulled across the dimensions.

If you stay quite conscious here, you can choose to cut or release these cords -- these umbilical cords – these ties to physical

and emotional bodies you are leaving. You can choose to cut these ties for yourself.[33] You can consciously give birth to yourself in the new form of yourself you are becoming.

You can consciously choose to deliver yourself. You can, at least conceptually, *deliver yourself* into a new dimension of your reality. You can give birth to your new self here. You can SEE BEYOND your physical plane and biological body's LINE OF SIGHT.

You can (develop within yourself the option to) *choose to extend onto your continuum of consciousness.*

---

[33] Discussion and exercises regarding these cords is offered in Volume 4 in this series, HOW TO DIE AND SURVIVE.

12
A Second Phase of Death

The previous chapter discusses letting go of physicality to "cross over." Crossing over is a variously defined event, varying for example based upon philosophical and or religious orientation.

Now, let's say here that when you reach this crossing over point, you have about completed the physical or at least medical death (depending on your own views of this process). Yet, in many philosophies and belief systems, there is more. Various views suggest that once you pass out of the body or physical vehicle, you have passed from the first episode of death or the first death, which is physical, to what can be called the second phase of death, which is not physical per se.

Non-Physical Body

In this next death comes the death of what can be described as the *non-physical body*, or in some jargons, the *energy body*, or perhaps the *emotional body* or *emotional vehicle*. Various labels for this body or vehicle are perhaps confusing. This reflects the vague nature, or the largely non-physical nature itself, of this "body."

How we define something, explain something, based on our physical plane measures, when this is not exactly a physical plane "thing," is of issue. We can at best only approximate what of ourselves is, or can be, beyond this physical plane or dimension. Our within-physical dimension tools and measures (and words) can only approximate *consciousness realities* they do not fully consciously reach into.

Emotional Body

When we think of the non-physical body, we are generally referring to what is frequently called the emotional body. This body is conceptually described as being within and around the physical body.

Many views claim that this emotional body is with us while we are alive, living in our physical bodies, and that this emotional body extends some distance around our physical bodies. Other views add that the emotional body may continue

SEEING BEYOND OUR LINE OF SIGHT

for a while (or in some instances live on for quite a while) after the physical body dies.

We can think in terms of the emotional body being formed by, and or forming, a web, a network, of energies, woven by the physical biological being. In terms of phases of death, the emotional body may live on as these energies or energy profiles may not entirely dissolve the moment the physical body dies. I leave it to Readers to decide for themselves their views on this.

What I do offer here is the suggestion that whatever is presently the case, whatever we presently believe we are or may be, *we have the opportunity to consciously develop, evolve ourselves beyond, what we presently are. In this sense, we have the opportunity to become aware of, even to expand upon, parts of ourselves that are not entirely physical, biological.*

We can SEE BEYOND, **even evolve ourselves to SEE further BEYOND**, OUR *present* LINE OF SIGHT.

As soon as we decide we do have an emotional body, we then of course may be confronted with the matter of the death of that body. And, as is the case for the first phase of death, the death of the biological body, this next phase of death may also

be quite profound. Yes, the death of the emotional body may be a profound death, as you have grown quite a complex emotional body during this physical biological lifetime.

When The Physical House Is Empty

Once the physical house of the body is truly empty, it begins to decompose. It may even begin to decompose before physical death takes place, which, when extreme, is the situation the dying person may not want to be tied to.

There is a distinct irony here. On the one hand, as noted earlier, cells may live on beyond the moment the body is declared medically dead, and on the other, the body may be decomposing before the body is pronounced medically dead.

The dying or shedding of cells, and the living on of the body, have taken place throughout the life of the body. We constantly shed skin cells, for example. Yet, as physical death comes, these processes may be ever more out of synch from a physical standpoint.

Every day, we are living and dying, this is all part of an ongoing process, the continuous transition.

Death May Not Be Complete

You may choose to think that death is complete at the physical end, after the stages of physical death described in previous chapters. This is certainly your option. Each of us decides for ourselves what we choose to believe, see, and know. We can each decide for ourselves how far beyond our physical bodies and our physical lifetimes we choose to reach, and how to prepare ourselves during our physical lifetimes to reach beyond.

For those who wish to consider additional possibilities along the *continuum of consciousness*, then additional steps and phases in this transition can be imagined or considered or even consciously explored.

Indeed Emotional Body Death

There may indeed be this next dying, that of the emotional body death or transition. For those who choose to consider the possibility of this movement, this expansion along the *continuum of consciousness* that this book describes, there are KEY ideas to explore.

If we can indeed imagine our consciousness being in existence beyond our biology, even perhaps free of biology, then this emotional body transition may be as much a great passage as physical death, if not more.

The individual who has just lost her or his physical body may still retain many of the ties to, or cords to, feelings and awareness-es of others' feelings acquired while in that physical biological body. I say *may* here, as there is much debate.

My view is that, no matter what the debate is regarding what presently is or may be, we have the option of further developing or evolving more. We can consciously choose to become ever more conscious of ourselves as not only biological beings. We can consciously choose to develop our own *continuum of consciousness* as our own *survival territory*.

In essence, we can at least conceptually, via our aware consciousness, extend our LINE OF SIGHT to beyond physical death. *We can conceptually live along an ongoing continuum of consciousness, rather than be confined to a defined biological lifespan.*

(Note: I repeat this matter several times in this book, as additional information and ideas are shared. I am thus

suggesting that, once we consider A, and then B, and so on, we again and again revisit the premise of this book, see further about how we can, and ideally will, SEE BEYOND OUR LINE OF SIGHT.)

We are already building bridges between this time, this "now," this physicality, and the realm beyond this physicality.

We are already expanding our *continuum of consciousness* so that it will be here for us when we choose to inhabit it. This is KEY in our own AFTER LIFE SUPPORT of ourselves as we choose to survive transitions and deaths.

The After Physical Death State

This book suggests that you have the option to understand yourself, to extend your awareness of yourself, into nonphysical realms. You can do this, you can reach beyond physical definitions of yourself, whether or not you have received intensive training.

This reaching will be an idea, a concept, you give your mind-brain to hold for you, to develop for you, to refine for you.

How this appears to you, how you form this idea of living beyond your physical body, will be personal to you.

Various belief systems, practices, and teachings may offer descriptions of such an option. Ultimately, for you to open this possibility in your mind, to have this option available to you when you may choose to call upon it, you will want to begin now. Yes, you can define, envision, explore, develop, personalize, *your own understanding of your own continuum of consciousness – and thus of your own survival options.*

You can do this **REACHING BEYOND** by consciously choosing to remain as conscious as you can during all your in-life and end-of-life transition and seeming death processes. You can get to know yourself, your awareness, in transition.

You can begin practicing this now, while you are biologically alive to read these words. Begin with the basic understandings in this book.

Also begin with these basic exercises: the *General Transition Awareness Exercise* following Chapter 3 in Part One of this book; and then the *Emotional Body Mapping Exercise* at the end of this present

chapter, and then the *Mental Body Mapping Exercise* at the end of the next chapter.

This Is About Staying With Your Personal Consciousness

Remember, this is not necessarily or only about staying biologically conscious. This is about holding on to *conscious awareness* in a form you learn to be ever more aware of—in your form. Start now. Explore your own out of body awareness-es and experiences. See what you sense and see, when out of your body for a moment, or for a brief time such as during a daydream or a sleeping dream, or during some other form of exercise or event.[34]

Of course, shedding an emotional body means letting go of a great deal of what may feel to be emotional baggage. Remember that all your emotional feelings are part of an emotional body that you are shedding.

Emotional bodies, while not as dense from a physical standpoint, are also quite dense. Here, density is not measured

---

[34] See other books in this series for *out of body experience* exercises. Also note, UNVEILING THE HIDDEN INSTINCT opens with a detailed look at various out of body experiences.

in terms of its physical characteristics per se. Rather, this density is conceptual, conceptually energetic, in terms of ties, cords, connections, entanglements, complexities of inter-weavings, and more. Readers know how emotionally complex and entangled their lives can be. We can get quite tied up, even caught in, emotional situations. We can even get trapped in these.

If you stay entangled in, even perhaps stuck and or trapped in, your emotional body, then your consciousness, energy, and power may distort or weaken during transitions. Those who do not clearly understand this second stage of death – what has been described as being emotional body death – may enter this transition anxious, or even fearful, angry, and or perhaps simply bewildered, and needlessly waste their consciousness' energy.

Try to take this information in by studying it from time to time. You will remember bits of this description many times during your livings and dyings. You may want to read more intricate reviews of the physical dying process than we have space for here.

Eventually, whatever her or his awareness, the physically dead individual must leave behind emotional connection to the

physical plane and move on. We can develop our understanding of what this means for us well in advance of this transition. We can speak to ourselves, get to know our emotional bodies while we live here in this physical plane with the physical bodies that are connected to those emotional bodies. (See the Emotional Body Mapping Exercise at the end of this chapter.)

Letting Go

This *letting go* is a critical and somewhat difficult process for many a conscious being or a consciousness.[35] In many ways, we may be more emotionally tied to emotional bodies then we may be to physical bodies. Resistance to this letting go is understandable.

At this point, the consciousness senses that what can come after emotional body death is yet another possible death, one that may be the dissipation of the mental body or non-emotional mental energy.

---

[35] See detailed discussion of this process of ***letting go***, of emotional body death and transition, in Volume 4 of this KEYS TO CONSCIOUSNESS AND SURVIVAL SERIES, titled HOW TO DIE AND SURVIVE, BOOK ONE.

CONSCIOUSLY MOVING THROUGH
LIFE'S CHANGES, TRANSITIONS, AND DEATHS

As discussed in the next chapter, we have the option of consciously developing for ourselves, while we are here living in physical biological bodies, our options. These are options we may then be able to consciously call upon at this later point in the dying process. This includes the ...

OPTION TO SURVIVE

BOTH HERE AND BEYOND.

Basic Emotional Body Mapping Exercise

Define and develop your sense of your emotional body. What follows is a useful exercise in the process of sensitizing yourself to your nonphysical realities, in this instance to what can be called your emotional body. Other books in this series provide additional exercises that build on this basic awareness....

1. Imagine you have an emotional body. Give this body a visual image. Draw or sketch this image. Give this image characteristics such as shape, location, texture, even lines or cords or ties to people or ideas, and ties to emotions themselves.

2. When you have an emotional experience, a feeling, form a sense of where this feeling is in your emotional body, and how this feeling looks and moves through your emotional body.

3. As you grow familiar with your emotional body, explore its variations. Does this emotional body ever change texture or shape or size? Does this body expand at times; does it recede at times? What affects this emotional body?

4. How close to your physical body is your emotional body located? Does this emotional body envelope or encircle the physical body? Does this emotional body reach into the physical body?

5. Can this emotional body move? Can it gain some distance from the physical body?

6. Try to move this emotional body a little distance away from your physical body. Can these two bodies separate? How tied to each other are these bodies?

7. What other characteristics can you look for to get to further know your emotional body?

13
A Third Phase of Death

This book explores the option we have to *choose to develop and stay in contact with our own awareness, and with our own personal consciousness itself,* as we move through in-life and seeming end-of-life transitions and deaths. However we have arrived at this juncture in our development, at this level of our awareness, we can choose to expand our awareness, to extend our *continuum of consciousness*. We can look BEYOND OUR presently known LINE OF SIGHT.

Leaving The Vehicle Behind

We can leave the physical and the emotional bodies, vehicles, and do so quite consciously. We can, in full waking awareness, preserve *our continuity of consciousness* while moving from the physical plane to the after-physical-death state or states. *We can continue to exist.*

Continue to exist? What will this look like, or be like? Here are some possible characteristics of this experience:

CONTINUE TO EXIST NOTES

1. If you imagine that you have left both your physical biological body and your emotional body, or have actually left these, your sensations, or better stated, awareness-es, will be experienced differently now. This will be a distinctly different experience from the physical and emotional body realities you have known.

2. Some sense of familiarity may be briefly experienced. There may be some similarities to near death and other out of body experiences the dying person may have had when living in a physical body.

3. Detachment may be felt, with a non-emotional sense of suspended self.

4. Initially, some brief confusion, or better stated, disorientation, may be felt. This sensation disappears very soon.

5. A sense of this new reality builds. A new validity, an additional sense that this suspended state is alright, and is indeed a reality, builds. (This is a little like moving into a new neighborhood, even a new house.)

6. A non-emotional awareness emerges, one saying that there may be no opportunity for waking up and falling back into your physical biological body, or even back into your emotional body. Acceptance of this is easy at this point.

7. The personal consciousness, personal awareness, may choose to experience parts of this as what seems to be sensory experience. This is alright. Reminders of physical sensations may arise as these sensations may be recalled and tagged to these new awareness-es. This is a little like translating a foreign language into one you know.

8. After a while, you know the language of your new reality, your new location along your continuum of consciousness. You will then need fewer reminders of previous sensations to understand what is taking place.

9. Moving into your nonphysical and non-emotional vehicle of your personal consciousness is taking place. As this is taking place, some trace ties to the physical and or emotional bodies may remain but be waning.

10. Without direct definitions of the elements of this non-physical and non-emotional experience, it may for a while still be identified with previous physical experience. For example, sensations of floating, of being weightless, of being outside and above the physical body, looking down on one's body, may appear.

11. Some further although non-threatening disorientation may still be experienced, as all this may continue to *seem to be* a new experience. However, emotions are not felt the way they are in the physical body, as biological mechanisms for emotions are diminishing or already gone. You will not have feelings as you once did.

12. Wait, just be with this experience. You will feel ever more at home here. This place will even feel familiar, as this is **_you_** being along and within **_your own_** continuum of consciousness, where you have already been existing. Meet your mental body. Welcome home.

SEEING BEYOND OUR LINE OF SIGHT

Detached Views Of Our SELVES

This is a KEY transition. Here, we have the option of being *aware* of our *self* as *consciousness,* and of maintaining ourself as a consciousness as we transition. Here is where we can SURVIVE.

As the previous chapters discuss, some views of our *selves* include not only the physical biological body, but some part of ourselves that is not entirely if at all physical. Some will call this the soul. Others will say this is the higher self. Others will suggest this is the consciousness. For the purposes of this book (and other books in this series), the term *personal consciousness* is used. This is to suggest that we can choose to remain ever more conscious as we move through transitions including deaths.

Previous chapters have discussed first and second phases of the death transition, and the option we have to consciously navigate these phases.

We also may have the option to consciously navigate through the first two phases into a next phase where we find what remains of us is the seeming mental body. Of course, regarding this third option, there is significant debate regarding the matter of whether the consciousness is biological or not biological. As noted in the Series Foreword at the opening to this book, this book suggests that we have the option to develop or further develop a level of ourselves that IS NOT TIED TO BIOLOGY. (See also the book, UNVEILING THE HIDDEN INSTINCT where this matter is further developed.)

Know The Mental Body

The mental body may be able to continue to survive after the emotional body has been shed.

It is said that very few spirits are so-called "evolved enough" to succeed in fully completing this third death and, in so doing, crossing the threshold beyond the death cycle. It is also said that most fail at this death and therefore must recycle as physical beings again and again until some day they will finally "succeed."

I certainly do not want to debate various teachings and belief systems. My view is that we each have the right to define these various phases of our lives and our deaths as we choose. I do suggest that we do our best to consider in depth *the possibility that there is still more to know beyond what we have been taught.*

SEEING BEYOND OUR LINE OF SIGHT

In terms of the belief that only the most so-called "evolved" of us have the so-called "option" of surrendering our mental bodies, I do have an alternative view. I suggest we think about this particular message. **I suggest we wonder what it means when we are told that the highest and best option is to surrender our mental body to a higher force.**

This message is not necessarily wrong. However, *the surrendering of one's mental energy must be studied closely.* **It may be that there are evolved consciousnesses, and also others of us who may still have yet to further evolve, who may** *consciously choose* **to retain our own mental body, to choose to have our personal aware consciousness SURVIVE.**

This may not be a less evolved choice, but rather an option we can realize we have. It appears that science and religion, and other belief systems, are not preparing us to recognize and exercise this option. (Again, I suggest the value of AFTERLIFE SUPPORT in helping us consciously navigate these realms of transition.)

We can allow ourselves to wonder about this mental death. When you die this third and final phase, is this actually final? If

so, where does your mental energy go? Where does your consciousness go? Where do you go? *Do you want to go there?* You can still have a say, you can STILL SURVIVE as a personal consciousness. *This is your right, your option, your opportunity.*

Discerning Options

Can it be that not all options are wonderful and safe? Can we learn in advance to discern when out of our physical bodies, to see what our options are? How far can we see, and how closely can we look, once we have seen, and ventured, and chosen to **stay conscious, BEYOND OUR LINE OF SIGHT?**

YOU HAVE A RIGHT TO DARE TO SURVIVE.

Are you willing to stay conscious right on through the death process in order to look closely at where you are sending your precious Human energy at this juncture? Do you know you may have the option of choosing what to do with your mental body?[36] DO YOU KNOW YOU HAVE THE OPTION OF

---

[36] An in depth look at this matter is offered in other books in this series, such as Volumes 4, 11, and 14, the HOW TO DIE AND SURVIVE books, and also Volume 3, UNVEILING THE HIDDEN INSTINCT.

SURVIVING? Question messages that have told you otherwise or have failed to inform you of this. (This questioning of authority even at this juncture may be KEY in survival.)

Navigating Death

You can ever more *consciously navigate your death* so as to be able to consciously choose the next destination, the place you choose to surrender your personal consciousness-- **IF YOU DO CHOOSE TO SURRENDER AND THEREFORE DIE.**

YOU ALSO CAN KNOW <u>YOU DO NOT HAVE TO DO SO</u>, that you can continue to survive without merging. **You can survive your physical death as a mental body living along your own continuum of consciousness.** This continuum is your actual home, and your actual survival vehicle, once you claim it. **This is where you actually do exist.**

CONSCIOUSLY MOVING THROUGH
LIFE'S CHANGES, TRANSITIONS, AND DEATHS

YES, YOU HAVE THE RIGHT TO DARE TO SURVIVE.

Also note that you can, while consciously navigating your death, avoid surrendering your mental energy -- to a force that may use it for other than you would freely choose to have it used. Each of us must assume responsibility for remembering this. We can choose to discern even at later junctures in our transitions.

If you can accept this responsibility, this awareness, you may be able to help free countless beings from being cycled against their wills through what may be the *Human energy plantation* and other farms and factories such as this one throughout the cosmos.[37]

On Navigating The Three Deaths ...

---

[37] See Volumes 5 and 6 in this series, titled, OVERRIDING THE EXTINCTION SCENARIO, Parts One and Two.

Consciously navigating the three deaths and beyond is the greatest opportunity for a being. Yet, this is an entirely natural, and in this sense, easy process.

CONSCIOUSLY SURVIVING TRANSITION IS POSSIBLE AND EVEN NATURAL.

Recognizing the major choice you have regarding your mental body, even regarding your personal consciousness itself, is essential. Being aware of your options helps to access them.

Reminding or guiding others who are undergoing physical death, whether or not medically conscious, can help these others access choices at death. On a broad population level, we may have been denied much of this awareness. Now is the time to take this awareness back.

And here is the metaphor: *navigating* the death process is navigating transition…. There is an art and a science AND A POLITIC of dying, of all transitioning, that we can learn and that we can apply to all types of transitions. (I have detailed this matter in the HOW TO DIE AND SURVIVE books, and also in UNVEILING THE HIDDEN INSTINCT.)

CONSCIOUSLY MOVING THROUGH
LIFE'S CHANGES, TRANSITIONS, AND DEATHS

A Question Of Rights

Your right to die in the manner and with the level of awareness you choose for yourself must be exercised while you are on Earth and in your physical body as well as in the time after you leave your physical body. Human rights extend far beyond the physical plane. You, as a personal consciousness, can exercise your rights there, if you so choose.[38] Human (Humanity's) rights extend far beyond the physical plane. Know your rights there, here.

*Now, let's step back from the metaphor of physical death to look at additional understandings we can build upon to be **ever more aware in the NAVIGATION of our lives**—understandings regarding where the boundaries between ourselves and our patterning and programming may be. NAVIGATING our lives, our changes, endings, deaths, **transitions**, involves **knowing ourselves, being conscious of**, who we are when we NAVIGATE....*

---

[38] This matter, **conscious phases of post-physical awareness** and travel, is defined and discussed more fully in other books in this KEYS TO CONSCIOUSNESS AND SURVIVAL SERIES.

SEEING BEYOND OUR LINE OF SIGHT

Basic Mental Body Mapping Exercise

Define and develop your sense of your mental body. This is a basic exercise in the process of further sensitizing yourself to your nonphysical realities, in this instance to what can be called your mental body. Other books in this series provide additional exercises that build on this basic awareness....

1. The idea of a mental body is a challenge to develop in that this body, in essence, has not only no physical characteristics, but also no emotional characteristics. The ideas in this basic exercise are a starting point to open the mind to consideration of the existence of the mental body.

2. To explore the notion of the mental body, imagine a part of your SELF that is not physical and not emotional. Give this part of your SELF a visual image. Draw or sketch this image. Just to work with the idea of your mental body, give this image characteristics such as shape, location, texture, etc.

3. Find something you can be aware of yet detached from, and not be responding to either physically or emotionally. Perhaps this is the idea of paper, or water, or what you can find that you are relatively neutral about. Focus on this. Give your awareness a sense of this sensation in order to track it. This awareness of this sensation is detached, distanced, separate, objective, whatever you find works for you here.

4. When you have found this awareness, this sensation of this thing you have selected, notice what your awareness seems to be. To explore this, give this awareness a location, a

characteristic, a texture, perhaps a movement state, and sketch this or make notes of this awareness.

5. As you grow familiar with your mental body, explore its variations if any. Does this mental body expand at times, does it recede at times? What if anything affects this mental body?

6. How close to, or separate from, your physical body and also to your emotional body is your mental body? Does this mental body envelope or encircle the emotional and or physical body? Does this mental body reach into the physical body?

7. Can this mental body move? Can it contract and expand? Can it gain some distance from the physical body and or from the emotional body?

8. Try to move this mental body a little distance away from your physical body, and then from your emotional body. Can these bodies separate? How tied to each other are these bodies?

9. What other characteristics can you look for to get to further know your mental body?

PART FOUR

CONTINUUM OF CONSCIOUSNESS

**CONSCIOUSLY MOVING THROUGH
LIFE'S CHANGES, TRANSITIONS, AND DEATHS**

14
Indistinct Boundaries Between Life And Death Shift To The Continuum

This book suggests we have the option of reaching BEYOND our given, or known, LINE OF SIGHT, expanding along what may be an extensive, or even an infinite, *continuum of consciousness*.

This very expansion speaks to death, says that death is not necessarily the finite ending that is commonly called death. Rather, death is a transition to a new state of being, or better stated, realization of an already existing state of being—or state of being *option.*

Boundary Between Physical Life And Death Is Increasingly Indistinct

Even time of death, time of physical death, is not distinct. There are several "official" times of physical body death: (a) the time recorded on a death certificate, which is generally said to be the legal time of death; (b) the time a medical examiner (who may not be present during the dying process itself) writes in his or her notes is the time of death; and, (c) the physiological time of death when medically-defined vital functions appear to cease.

Were we tracking time of physical death in ever more detail, we might also measure the time when each and every cell in the body is finally dead, which is frequently a time much later than the above noted time of death measures. Some cells can outlive the physical body for days and even weeks. This suggests that actual physical death is not as distinct as we have previously thought it to be. When we speak of physical death, we must ask: physical death when, and physical death of what, and why these are the measures being applied.

Recent findings are bringing, even forcing, the entire time of death issue under reconsideration. Studies are now showing that within some cells that are living on past the medical time of death, there have been found unexpected genetic activities appearing in these cells. Actual increases in the transfer activity of many cells' messenger RNA molecules is taking place following given time of death. Post mortem changes in genes are opening up whole new questions about whether the body lives

on, or parts of the body live on, and whether this can be applied to bring someone back to "life."

This entire issue of *cellular afterlife* is threatening to upset medical theory regarding end of life. When is the physical, biological, body actually dead? What new approaches might be taken to allow this life to be functionally extended? Is biological brain death always the best determinant? What does this say about the death *or the survival of the consciousness itself*? What might be done to contribute to the survival of the awareness, the aware consciousness, itself?

The Boundary Between Physical End-of Life And Life Beyond Physicality May Be Increasingly Indistinct

We will continue to discover more about the possible and even actual survival of life following the death of the body.

Research findings are revealing that some of the cells that live on following the death or seeming death of the physical body appear to behave like, or better stated revert to behavior of, cells similar to those of cells in embryos.

Also note that scientists are finding no explanation for cases where brain waves continue for some time following the

time some patients are removed from life support and pronounced dead. These are not what are termed "death waves" seen in laboratory study of dead animals. Rather, these are delta waves, found in living people, generally during deep sleep.

The boundary between, and even definition of, life and death is evolving. Not only is this the result of ongoing scientific findings, *this is also the result of our own species expansion along our own continuum of consciousness. On some level, even perhaps instinctively, we are sensing this is an option, a survival-related option, we do have. Thus, we are already expanding into our rightful place along this continuum.*

Boundaries Between One's Own Deaths May Be Indistinct

The previous chapters discuss actual physical death as both a model of and a metaphor for transition processes. Death, as any transition, moves through stages of change, which are stages of transition itself. Of course, stages of transition beyond the death of the physical body have still to be more closely mapped. (<u>Many of us are working on this map now</u>.[39])

The moment of delineation of death is ever less distinct once we extend the idea of physical death to include the death of what may be additional and less physical bodies. Once the boundary between what we consider biological life and what we call biological death blurs, then physical death itself may be less absolute and ever more *transitional*.

Previous chapters discuss the concept and even possibility that we may have additional bodies such as less than, or other than, entirely physical bodies, and perhaps even entirely non-physical bodies. Some of these bodies have been described as the "emotional body" and the "mental body."

Whether or not we believe we presently have these partially *or entirely* non-physical bodies, this book suggests that

---

[39] Certainly, there have been religious and spiritual pathways suggested, such as those offered by the Tibetan Book of the Dead, and other doctrines. This present book, SEEING BEYOND OUR LINE OF SIGHT, and other books in this KEYS TO CONSCIOUSNESS AND SURVIVAL SERIES, offer additional views, mappings, and pathways not associated with particular doctrines or philosophies per se, and open the door to development of more details regarding the transitional experiences we may face when leaving the physical body.

we have the *option of developing these* by consciously extending our LINE OF SIGHT. Our consciousness has the option of defining and extending itself across its *continuum of consciousness*, reaching well BEYOND OUR biologically based LINE OF SIGHT.

Our individual as well

as species survival

may at some time even depend upon this.[40]

---

[40] In depth discussion of the *survival value of this awareness* is included in the OVERRIDING THE EXTINCTION SCENARIO books, which are Volumes 5 and 6 in this series.

15
Introduction To The Continuum Of Consciousness

The following charts and diagrams are offered to suggest questions regarding:

1. Where we are, together, and as individuals, along what this book defines as the *continuum of consciousness*.

2. Whether we can ever more consciously and purposefully move in and out of levels of consciousness, or levels of access to our own consciousness, in response to what is taking place within and around us.

3. How we may be able to have significant say in where we are along this *continuum of consciousness*.

This book (as do other books in this KEYS TO CONSCIOUSNESS AND SURVIVAL SERIES) suggests that, no matter how we got here, and no matter where we believe we

presently are along the *continuum of consciousness,* we have the *option of shifting ourselves to greater degrees of awareness, of consciousness, both in this physical place, and beyond this physical plane.*

We can develop, evolve, an ever greater capacity to reach beyond, perhaps to live BEYOND, OUR LINE OF SIGHT. The more we recognize our capacity to reach BEYOND OUR given physical plane LINE OF SIGHT, the more we SEE that we can reach BEYOND, live beyond, our current and perhaps limiting, LINE OF SIGHT.

SEEING BEYOND OUR LINE OF SIGHT

16
The Maze Of Consciousness

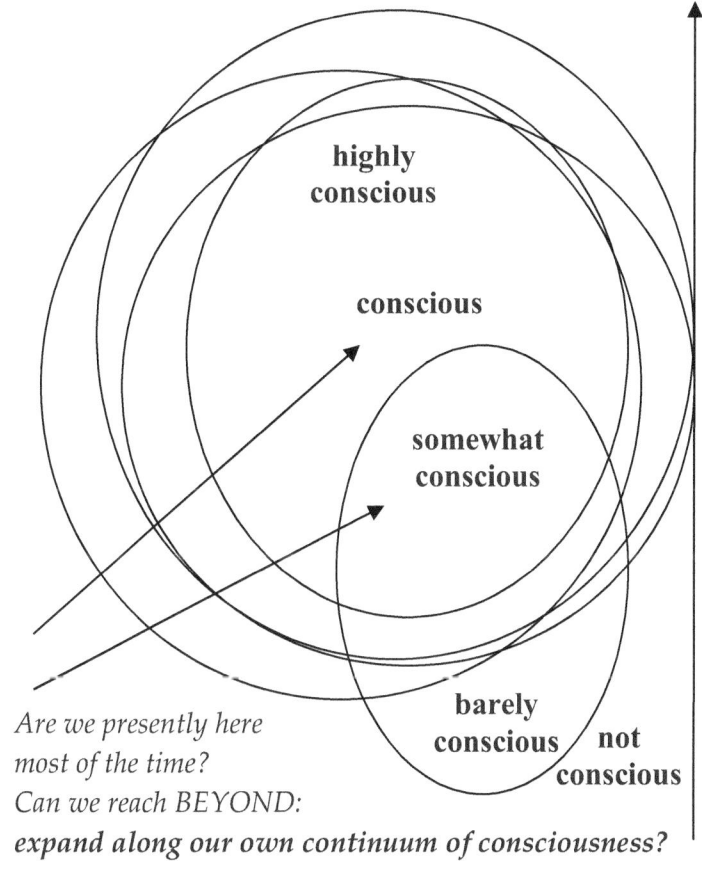

Are we presently here most of the time?
Can we reach BEYOND:
expand along our own continuum of consciousness?

**CONSCIOUSLY MOVING THROUGH
LIFE'S CHANGES, TRANSITIONS, AND DEATHS**

17
Overlapping Levels Of Perceived Consciousness

The Continuum of Consciousness

not → barely → somewhat → more → highly
conscious   conscious   conscious   conscious   conscious

Where are we along this continuum of consciousness
in daily "waking" life?

Where do we think we are in daily "waking" life?

Where do we appear to others to be in daily "waking" life?

Where do we appear to others to be
when in various stages of physical death?

Where do we appear to ourselves to be
when in various stages of physical death?

We are so much more than meets the eye.

Who we are and where we are is
something the physical eye may not tell us.

What dies when the physical body dies?

What does not have to die?

Where can we go along this continuum of consciousness?

**CONSCIOUSLY MOVING THROUGH
LIFE'S CHANGES, TRANSITIONS, AND DEATHS**

18
The Many Deaths…

Physical, biological, death involves stages of the *separation of the **life of the being** from the physical body*, with a common pattern of physical death described on the following pages.

Following physical (biological) death, what may be called non-biological death or *transition* typically involves departing the physical body, and then perhaps departing what is sometimes described as the emotional body, and then perhaps moving into other bodies that are not necessarily biologically-based, such as the mental body … Even these non-biologically-based bodies may be retained or shed.

It may be that we can develop the capability to retain our consciousness through the various in-life and seeming end-of-life transitions. It may be that we can develop ourselves to be increasingly aware as we move through our *continuum of consciousness*. →→→→

CONSCIOUSLY MOVING THROUGH
LIFE'S CHANGES, TRANSITIONS, AND DEATHS

The diagram pictured on the following page indicates phases of death (biological, emotional, and mental) as follows.

Note that three *stages* of the biological death *phase* are described. There are many explanations of the biological death process, and Readers who are interested are encouraged to read more on this process. This is simply a summary.

Note that the following diagram also suggests that:

- After the biological death phase,
  the next phases relate to the so-called
  emotional body and then the so-called mental body.

- In what has been called the emotional body death,
  this emotional body has been formed by and entangled with the physical body, brain, and nervous system:
  This body requires its own death to be shed.

- Next is the death **or survival -- I suggest we may be able to further develop this option for continuing on as what has been called the mental body, or as**
  the personal consciousness.
  Here, this mental body grows ever less and then not at all entangled with the emotional and the physical (biological) bodies.
  This mental body, or personal consciousness itself
    may be able to
    ever more consciously survive:
    THIS IS THE QUESTION
          (OR OPTION) OF THE HOUR....

SEEING BEYOND OUR LINE OF SIGHT

**Higher,
non-physical, (such as so-called mental or even personal consciousness) bodies,
now free of ties to biological and even emotional bases,
may be able to ever more consciously survive.**

THREE STAGES OF A COMMON BIOLOGICAL DEATH

Stage One:
Body begins to shut down.
Biologically based consciousness begins to recede.
Brain sucks up sugar and oxygen from the body.
Brain hangs on to biological consciousness in some form, typically flashing back, releasing memories in a stream of rushes.

Stage Two:
Brain goes into high drive, with pulsating brain waves, starving the body.
High state of non-emotional bliss experienced by brain.

Stage Three:
Body stops breathing, seeing. Any remaining physical sensations end.
Last words, if any, have been uttered by now.

AFTER BIOLOGICAL DEATH,
NEXT PHASE OF DEATH MAY BE:
EMOTIONAL BODY, which is
IS ENTANGLED WITH PHYSICAL BODY, BRAIN
AND NERVOUS SYSTEM:
Requires its own death to be shed.

MENTAL BODY NOT ENTANGLED,
can choose to survive.

**CONSCIOUSLY MOVING THROUGH
LIFE'S CHANGES, TRANSITIONS, AND DEATHS**

SEEING BEYOND OUR LINE OF SIGHT

19
We Need Not Die

> **Phase One: PHYSICAL/BIOLOGICAL BODY DEATH**
> **Physical/biological death** involves the stages of the separation of the life of the being from the physical body, with a common pattern of physical death proceeding as in the three phases of biological death listed below:
>
> **Stage One: Biological Body Death**
> Body begins to shut down.
> Biologically based consciousness begins to recede.
> Brain sucks up sugar and oxygen from the body.
> Brain hangs on to biological consciousness in some form, typically flashing back,
> releasing memories in a stream of rushes.
>
> **Stage Two: Biological Body Death**
> Brain goes into high drive, with pulsating brain waves, starving the body.
> High state of non-emotional bliss experienced by brain.
>
> **Stage Three: Biological Body Death**
> Body stops breathing, seeing. Any remaining physical sensations end.
> Last words, if any, have been uttered by now.
>
> **Next Phase: EMOTIONAL BODY DEATH**
> Emotional body is entangled with physical body, brain, and nervous system:
> Requires "astral" or other death to be shed.
> Mental body not entangled.
>
> **Next Phase: MENTAL BODY NEED NOT DIE**
> **Non-biological death** can include the mental body. However, the mental body can free itself from ties to biological death to **survive transition.**
> Transition typically involves departing the physical body, and the emotional body, and moving into bodies (if any) which are not biologically-based.
>
> **These non-biologically-based bodies and their patterns may be retained or shed,**
> **MAY BE CONSCIOUSLY RETAINED OR SHED.**

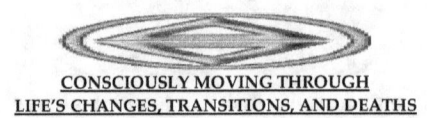
**CONSCIOUSLY MOVING THROUGH
LIFE'S CHANGES, TRANSITIONS, AND DEATHS**

20
Transcending Physicality And Its Patterns

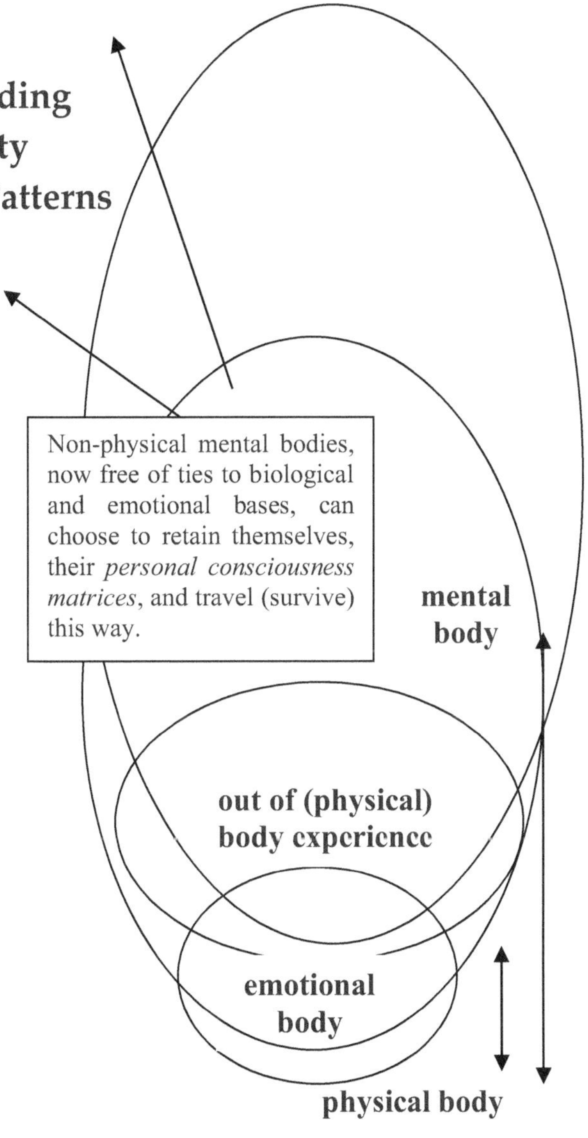

> Non-physical mental bodies, now free of ties to biological and emotional bases, can choose to retain themselves, their *personal consciousness matrices*, and travel (survive) this way.

mental body

out of (physical) body experience

emotional body

physical body

**CONSCIOUSLY MOVING THROUGH
LIFE'S CHANGES, TRANSITIONS, AND DEATHS**

PART FIVE

Mastering Transition Along
The Continuum Of Consciousness

**CONSCIOUSLY MOVING THROUGH
LIFE'S CHANGES, TRANSITIONS, AND DEATHS**

21
Master Transition From One Reality To Another

This chapter formulates in-life and seeming end-of-life changes, transitions, as being the *shifting of the self, of the awareness, along the personal continuum of consciousness.*

We carry a great deal of untapped knowledge about who we are and what our actual capacities are, or can be, *or can be consciously developed to be.* **It is possible that much of this knowledge has been suppressed within us, perhaps even structurally denied us.**[41]

The awareness-es, intuitive abilities, and *consciousness technologies* described in these KEYS TO CONSCIOUSNESS AND SURVIVAL books can be developed and applied to *conscious survival of transitions.*

---

[41] See discussion of this matter in other books in this KEYS TO CONSCIOUSNESS AND SURVIVAL SERIES, such as Volume 5 titled, OVERRRIDING THE EXTINCTION SCENARIO, and Volume 3 titled, UNVEILING THE HIDDEN INSTINCT.

We can develop our awareness of our capabilities to survive while living here in the physical plane. These are awareness-es, capabilities, intuitive abilities, and *consciousness technologies* that we can apply to navigating even physical plane conditions and problems.

Note that these awareness-es and abilities to navigate, and even to survive, may continue to be, on some level, (unintentionally and or intentionally) withheld from the general species population. This blocking of our conscious access to what we have a right to consciously know is a generally invisible issue. Yet, however this knowledge exists, this knowledge is every person's birthright.[42]

Why This Esoteric Discussion?

You are being invited to rethink death just a little bit, because you are a far more potent being than many teachers of history, science, and religion may have told you. You are so expansive a being that your energy field already touches many

---

[42] See discussion of this birthright in the books, HOW TO DIE AND SURVIVE, and also OVERRIDING THE EXTENCTION SCENARIO, and also UNVIELING THE HIDDEN INSTINCT.

states of reality, many arrangements of energy, many dimensions of your self, of your consciousness itself. In fact, you are in contact with and living within many dimensions at once, right here. You exist within and along the multidimensional matrix we can call the *continuum of consciousness*, which is already right here.

Right here? You might wonder where else you could really be while you are right here. *Right here* is an elusive concept, even though this sounds concrete. In reality, there is no more of a *right here* here than there is anywhere else. Basically, the sense of location you have is colored by your tie to your physical reality. This physicality is only one dimension of your existence. There are many other dimensions or arrangements of energy. Many of those dimensions are already all *right here*. This is true because you, everyone, exists in a *matrix of dimensions* within varying degrees of physical and non-physical reality.[43]

Some of you are now asking, "But then, why can't I *see* these other dimensions of our own awareness, of our own

---

[43] This matrix is detailed in depth in the book, UNVEILING THE HIDDEN INSTINCT.

consciousness?" The answer is that you *can* see or better stated, *sense*, these, but perhaps not the way you usually see or sense things.

You do see yourself immersed in time passing (perhaps by age-ing, perhaps by watching a child grow up) and in distance traveled (perhaps on the freeway or a plane flight). And, you will see much more when you learn to not only be using your physical eyes as the ultimate arbiters of reality, when you retrain your optic nerve and develop your third eye.

Everything is right here, whether or not you can see it. Start looking with all your senses, with all your awareness-es.

Dimensions Of Reality

Everyday life has many faces. Even within the limited physical dimension realities in which many of us have been told we live, there are many realities. Energy is always arranging and rearranging. Every second, our bodies and our minds are at least slightly different than they were a second ago.

Take some time to think about this -- to let this concept become a part of you: the concept of *death as a transition of, or*

relocation of, energy from one arrangement of itself, from one reality, to another.

Sometimes this transition must travel through several realities or aspects of realities to reach a resting point, the new reality the transition is seeking.

Now take some time to think about *this* -- to let *this* concept become a part of you: the concept of *death as a transition of, or relocation of, YOUR CONSCIOUSNESS* from one aspect of itself to another along your *continuum of consciousness.*

Sometimes this *TRANSITION OF THE CONSCIOUSNESS* must travel through several of its realities or aspects of its realities to reach a new resting point, the new reality that the consciousness is seeking.

Navigating The Concept Of Transition

You can learn to recognize, to be ever more aware of, a *conscious transition* and therefore a *conscious rearrangement of your SELF in transition.* This enhanced awareness you can apply to all your transition processes, whatever the level of transition may be -- whether it is a transition out of a state of mind, or a behavior,

a relationship, a habit such as a drug addiction, or an illness, or a physical body in the case of biological death. Think of all your changes as being shifts from one state of your awareness, of your reality, to another.

The following discussion will help loosen any rigid perceptions of reality that may keep you from further knowing this. Allow these ideas to flow into your mentality without working at taking them in. Remember that this discussion is basically telling you that you CAN learn to *consciously rearrange your SELF, your awareness*. You CAN break free of an energy pattern or arrangement in which you may feel you are held, caught, confined, or even trapped. You can break free of a perception of energy, perception of a pattern, in which you feel you are existing, or suspended, or perhaps caught.

Use the imagination function of your mind-brain. Allow yourself to explore what this means. Allow yourself to SEE BEYOND your LINE OF SIGHT, to expand along the *continuum of your consciousness*. Imagination can be a way to allow your brain and mind, your aware consciousness itself, to open new areas of inquiry, to discover new avenues, to further define itself.

SEEING BEYOND OUR LINE OF SIGHT

While we live here in our physical bodies, every one of our thoughts and ideas transmits itself through the biological brain. Micro-level brain activity is always taking place. New pathways are always being suggested and explored.

Training the mind to become more aware of the personal consciousness, to speak to the personal consciousness, is a **KEY** *conscious transition practice.*

22
Imagination For Exploration Of Transition Situations

This chapter takes a moment to speak to the visceral and creative self, the more intuitive regions of the mind-brain. Here, the idea of survival across phases and stages of in-life and seeming end-of-life transition is shared as a journey, a travel through ideas, concepts, states of mind. This chapter speaks ever more in the form of metaphor to call on the creative mind to further explore transition.

Imagination As Tool

Imagination can be a tool of discovery, an exercise of the brain, the mind, and the consciousness, to discover, explore, and expand pathways of awareness. Imagination can exercise the awareness, can strengthen the awareness.

Important note here: Certainly, imagination itself does not produce fact per se. For example, simply because you imagine

you can fly does not mean you should jump off a building assuming you can fly.

In the instance of this book, imagination is suggested as a *tool for developing awareness of the possibilities and capabilities of conscious non-physical expansion.*

[Note: Some Readers have said that this sort of thing can also be explored via psychoactive medication and or drugs. While this particular book does not offer an opinion on those methods, what this book does say is that the mind exploring the expansion of the mind, of the consciousness, does best to explore as below unaided by outside chemicals or materials. ... This allows for unaided authentic *conscious exercise of the consciousness.* This allows for the unaided authentic retention of this exercise for *conscious recall under unforeseen conditions that may be encountered in later seeming after-life transition experiences (such as those when there may be no physical body to drug, medicate, or treat in other ways).*]

Sample Transition Exploration

So here, let's use this imagination function to have the aware consciousness explore itself in the following sample of

imagined transition in what may be called "later stages of death."... Note again that this is the mind using the imagination to explore *transition realms and transition passages* that are not readily described in words. Therefore, these words only approximate here:

EXPLORE MOBILITY

Let's start with the idea of mobility. Sensing yourself, your S-E-L-F, as an awareness rather than a physical body is a beginning. Now, sensing your SELF as an *awareness that is mobile*, that can move itself, that can shrink or expand or travel in other ways, is good practice.

This begins to fine tune the awareness, the aware consciousness, to itself and to its *capacity to survive transition as itself*.[44] This *capacity to survive* is one that *survives as an awareness, as an aware consciousness*. Developing a strong and conscious connection to one's personal awareness during one's physical lifetime greatly contributes to conscious survival later.

---

[44] See definition of and exercises for this AWARE CONSCIOUSNESS in Volume 3, UNVEILING THE HIDDEN INSTINCT.

SEE THE EYE OF THE NEEDLE

Think about the notion of contraction and expansion of your *presence*, of your *aware consciousness*. Let's give this concept ideas that can help us imagine this:

You can shrink down or evaporate (your choice) and pass through what feels to the mind to be something like the *eye of the needle*, and then *expand right into the relief* of what may seem to be space. You can come and go from that space, to and from that sort of hyperspace, to and from other dimensions, other vibrational levels of reality, anytime you choose. It is your right to be able to move your *self*, your mind, your awareness, around this way.

MOVE THROUGH

Imagine that this *moving or passing through* is a way to *consciously navigate, consciously survive, a minor or major transition,* and even a calamity-like event, (calamity which is also a transition from the time before the calamity through the time of the calamity to the time following the calamity).

SEEING BEYOND OUR LINE OF SIGHT

In a passage, even a challenging transition that may feel like death, you can envision passing right through the so-called eye of the needle into another arrangement of your SELF. In fact, even calamity, apocalypse, whether it is an apocalypse which is all in your mind or body, or a natural disaster such as an earthquake, or some other event, is often the reason for *reaching through the eye toward the beyond*, SEEING BEYOND THE LINE OF SIGHT.

REACH BEYOND

The BEYOND is, simply, a place where your energy can be more free of the physical plane formed patterns, even any detrimental patterns, that were holding it, confining it, perhaps trapping it, perhaps even draining it, even if those detrimental patterns were patterns within or OF your physical body.

KNOW WINDOWS

Everywhere around and within us are *opportunities for movement, for passage through, and in and out of,* energy arrangements, realities, beyond our current patternings. It is important to be able to detect, to sense, to find these passages -- these windows, these eyes of these needles.

DETECT WINDOWS OF OPPORTUNITY

These *windows of opportunity* are windows into other situations, energy arrangements, realities.

These opportunities, these openings, are all around you, but remain hidden until you train yourself to see, sense, them.[45]

With practice, you will find your windows. Yes, these are *windows of opportunity* although they may appear, at first, if you can spot them at all, to be escape hatches.

TRAVEL THROUGH WINDOWS

You can move through these windows by imagining or actually becoming what you visualize as very, very small or compact, or by becoming so very spread out, vast, that you have no physical (or conceptual) density.

SHIFT YOURSELF

Remember that you can shift your idea of your *self*. For example, you can imagine becoming very dense – reducing down into a sort of *nowhere-ness*, or you can spread very thin –

---

[45] See the description of *navigating windows of opportunity* and other elements of transition in BOOK TWO of NAVIGATING LIFE'S STUFF.

expanding into a sort of *everywhere-ness*. This reduction and or expansion is your own choice. It is your choice, at any moment that you have available to you, to consciously employ (imagine) these choices (or not to).

Just imagine yourself into the form you choose. Imagination is quite powerful in this way. Imagination offers your consciousness great flexibility and versatility.

> **Imagination can become
> a way to fine tune one's
> navigation awareness.**

Dimension-Shifting May Feel To Be Like Death

So, moving your aware consciousness from one sense of your reality, of your SELF, to another is a type of transition, a form of in-life and or seeming end-of-life pattern shift or change or death. All death, including in-life transition in which there is no physical death, can be compared to this process. The experience will vary depending on the circumstances, and in some instances, your preparation for it.

BE AWARE OF SENSATIONS

Certainly the sensation of the mouth filling with cement, (as described in earlier chapters), may be a sensation coming with the passage of the self (of the awareness) into non-physical reality. Certainly there are other sensations that can accompany moving the self through dimensions, such as euphoria, bliss, floating, unweighting, disorientation, or sensations of shift, or perhaps what seems to be energy (or your *self*) rearranging.

SENSE TRAVELING THROUGH

For example, you may feel you are traveling through what seem to be very soft sheets of glass, softly shattering or dissolving each of these sheets as you move, and then being propelled by the force of that soft shattering still deeper through the glass sheets, which continue to shatter and dissolve as you proceed.

You may, for very brief a moment, feel that you cannot see. Just give yourself a moment, as **this is the eye of your awareness adjusting.**

SEEING BEYOND OUR LINE OF SIGHT

You may very briefly feel as if you cannot breathe, perhaps that you are momentarily trapped. This sensation fades as you quickly realize you are not a physical being; so these reminders of old physical sensations are gone or going away soon.

The closed-in or trapped feeling is generally so fleeting it goes by unnoticed. If some vague tie to the emotional body is still present, perhaps even some vague connection to a vague emotion such as a vague fear is present, these sensations dissolve very soon.

In the process of letting go, shifting to new formats of yourself, of your awareness, you may be fluctuating in your sense of what is taking place. This fluctuation is brief. You may feel a temporary sense of (what you interpret as) compression, perhaps feeling momentarily compressed to what feels like complete flatness. However this is a *dimension shift sensation* that is gone almost before it is noticed.

KNOW THIS IS A PASSING SENSATION

If you find yourself amidst such experiences, know these are generally quite brief, even momentary. These are merely passing sensations; this can be merely the passage to a new state.

Let time pass. After a while, you may sense what appear to be welcome, perhaps soft, flat sheets of fluid light fly out of the dark, like soft pieces of broken glass with no sharp edges. Imagine that you become one of those pieces of fluid light.

THINK OF THIS AS SOFT SHATTERING

Let yourself do what you may have no way to describe, except perhaps to think of this as soft fluid shattering or dissolving, the *self* **RE-forming** itself. *Feel you are breaking apart from your old holding pattern, from your old structure.* If you feel no relief when you shatter or dissolve, if you still feel compressed toward a flatness, hang in there. This sensation washes away almost immediately.

Release any lingering ties or cords to your physical and emotional bodies, if you sense these are present. This release will ease your passage, facilitate your transition.

TAKE ON A FLUIDITY

If you feel flat-ish, let yourself be flat. As you do, take on a fluidity to your flatness: sense that you are moving as part of the surface of a body of water, the top of the lake or a sea. You can

sense you are moving within a moving surface. Allow, even look for, motion of your self, as this facilitates your sense of mobility, *the mobility and survivability of your awareness, of YOU.*

SEE THIS AS A LAUNCH PAD

This is one of many possible experiences of *shifting the self, the awareness, the consciousness, through dimensions of itself, of changing energetic form.* This particular experience is a bit like a launch pad. You are perhaps moving to one arrangement of yourself to spring from it to another. In this case, you may be accepting your momentary, brief, reduction to what may feel to be a two dimensional or somehow flat form.

SHAPE SHIFT TO MOVE THROUGH

You are shape-shifting. Your awareness, your aware consciousness, is shifting its form to move through the eye of the needle, through the window into your passage, into and through your transition.

You are doing this as consciously as you can. As you do, you find you are surviving.

While you are accepting your brief reduction to what seems to be a two dimensional form, you will remember this description. You will know that the flatness, the temporary compression you may feel, is merely a passing state (unless you choose to stay in that compressed form).

PASS THROUGH FLATNESS

Should you have such an experience, you are doing something like this passing through the flatness of a temporarily reduced reality. This may seem to be two dimensional reality, where everything exists on a plane. But, even as this is happening to you, you may cling to your 3-D earthly views of reality. You may have little sense that you are compressing in order to launch yourself, THAT YOU ARE EXERCISING YOUR MOBILITY.

MOVE BEYOND A 3-D SITUATION

In terms of *cross-dimensional awareness, transition and travel*, you can say that you are launching your awareness, your aware consciousness, from the third dimensional (3-D), the physical plane base, into the second dimension in order to move into the fourth dimension and escape a 3-D physical plane pattern issue,

perhaps a possible or actual physical (or emotional) problem on the third dimensional level.

You may do this instinctively. However, it is best for you to do this shifting of the self, of the *personal consciousness*, as consciously as you are ready to. *This is you consciously surviving.*

Choose to hold on to your awareness, hold on to the focus of your awareness as being your personal consciousness, as being YOU, your identity, through all this.[46]

You can consciously choose to consciously survive this and all your transitions. You can expand to locate your awareness, and therefore your SELF, along your *continuum of consciousness*.

IF YOU FIND YOURSELF IN DARKNESS, WAIT

If you find yourself in darkness, wait. Time is not what you have known it to be. This sense of waiting is both long and very brief. This darkness is a rapidly passing *transitional sensation*.

---

[46] See exercises for *holding this focus* in Volume 3, UNVEILING THE HIDDEN INSTINCT.

WATCH FOR THE LIGHT

Remember that a magnificent stream of glistening light will wash through the dark flatness. See this light. Ride this light. When you feel air, or something like air, rush into what you feel to be your lungs, you will realize with relief that **you are not really dead. Instead of dying, you have just traveled along your** *continuum of consciousness.*

You have survived.

JUST CROSSED THRESHOLD/S

You have just crossed one or more thresholds into a new arrangement of your being, of your consciousness, of your awareness....

Dimensional Awareness And Travel

You may have sensed you had become a reflection, a reflection of your three-dimensional self. Becoming flat, two dimensional, is one way to move into the fourth dimension, the fourth dimension where time travel is the typical form of motion

SEEING BEYOND OUR LINE OF SIGHT

(similar to the way travel around town or around the planet is typical three dimensional travel).

The third dimension, the material plane, is located toward what we can call (from our material plane perspective) the "middle" of the multiple dimensions of reality. If you want to move up a dimension, to move around in time, either backward or forward, you may first have to move your energy "down" a dimension (as described above).

EVERYDAY PRACTICE

All of the above is an exercise in metaphor. There are various metaphors to think of here, from a conceptual or an awareness standpoint.

For example, one creative picture is that, if you, your mind, your consciousness, *can learn to do this well while still living in a physical body*:

> You may be able to, if still maintaining a physical body, return from this springboard, from this **conceptual time and dimension-shift.**

This particular shift is about leaping down to the second dimension, from there bouncing up to the fourth, and then landing back in the third dimension -- to return back to the third dimension with your body intact (and even with the clothes you had on when you left).

You can do this via your focus, your attention center focus, if you choose to.

This, after all, is what you just now thought through as you read this chapter, and you are still here, aren't you? ... As you have never left the physical form of yourself, as you are only moving the *focus of your consciousness*: you are still living in a physical body at this time.

Or, perhaps with practice, you can indeed affect your physical condition by working on your energy arrangements from a short distance outside yourself, from a different perspective, from elsewhere along your *continuum of consciousness*. (See other books in this series regarding this DE-

and then RE- SOMATIZATION process, such as Volume 3, UNVEILING THE HIDDEN INSTINCT.)

ABOUT MOVING YOUR FOCUS

You can practice this in everyday life, while living in a physical body. If you are able to *move your focus outside your physical body* for a little while, you can then return to your physicality which is still there waiting for you. Each time you do this temporary shifting of focus, you will be a little more aware of your great capacity to SEE BEYONG YOUR present biological LINE OF SIGHT.

In everyday life, temporarily raising one's focus, one's awareness, to beyond physicality, to a less dense form, can even allow for slight amendments, rearrangements, restructurings, of energy arrangements, which can then be moved back down to the physical plane.

Consider Dimensions Of Energy

As you master the use of your *aware consciousness*, and raise the *power of your consciousness*, you will have more ability to ever more *consciously navigate* your in-life and seeming end-of-life transitions. Mastering the dying process -- or transitional passage -- makes life ever more worth living.

In fact, the more the awareness can consciously envision and even master its own mobility and thus in-life and seeming end-of-life transitions, the more fully life can be lived.

23
Shifting The Self Through Transition

Moving through forms, levels, dimensions of one's reality is of course conceptual, an idea or image formed in the mind. And this is the focus of this book: what the mind, the awareness, can consciously develop, focus on, and move itself through.

We can become ever more in touch with the *consciousness functions* of not only our physical brain, but of what of these functions may be able to bring us, reach us, expand us, via imagination or visualization or other skills of the consciousness, beyond physicality. In so doing, the aware consciousness may be able to *consciously extend* BEYOND our present LINE OF SIGHT.

In speaking to our mind, to our metacognition, and then to our consciousness itself, we can share our sense that we do exist along a *continuum of dimensions of ourselves* where our *continuum of consciousness* resides. We can follow this understanding to consider more about shifting our form from one dimension of ourselves to another. ***This can be transition rather than death.***

CONSCIOUSLY MOVING THROUGH
LIFE'S CHANGES, TRANSITIONS, AND DEATHS

Let's pause a moment to remind ourselves of physical plane dimensions we know....

First there is the dimensionless point,
the zero dimension:

And then, this point, when extended,
forms a line, a row of points.

This line represents the first dimension,
because it has only one dimension, length.

When you drag that line, you have a row of lines, or a plane:

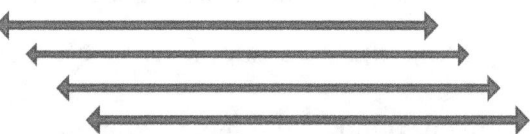

This row of lines forms this two dimensional plane:

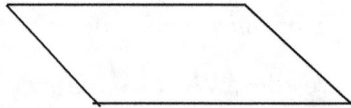

This is the second dimension,
as this has these two dimensions, length and width.

SEEING BEYOND OUR LINE OF SIGHT

Now, when you drag this plane through space,
you get something with depth.
This is thus three dimensional reality,
which you may believe know quite well:

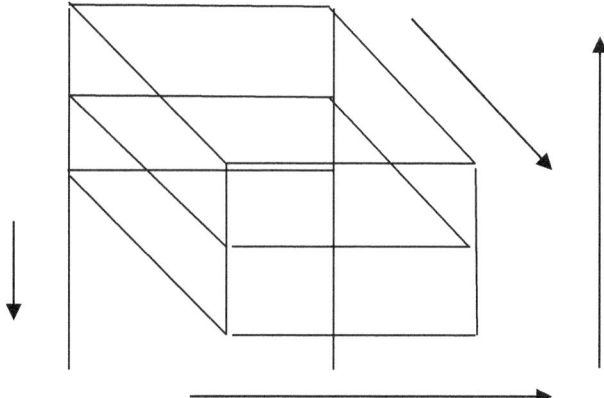

The arrows in the above diagram begin to suggest to us that we are living in more than only a 3-D reality. Living in a physical body, one which ages over time, you physically exist primarily on the border of the third and fourth dimension.

Any three dimensional life form moving through time is, to some degree, traveling in the fourth dimension. But the agility of that life form's travel is a bit hampered by its ties to its third dimensional structure, the physical body in which it lives.

CONSCIOUSLY MOVING THROUGH
LIFE'S CHANGES, TRANSITIONS, AND DEATHS

So we are, while in physical bodies,
in bodies that are 3-D yet moving through time:

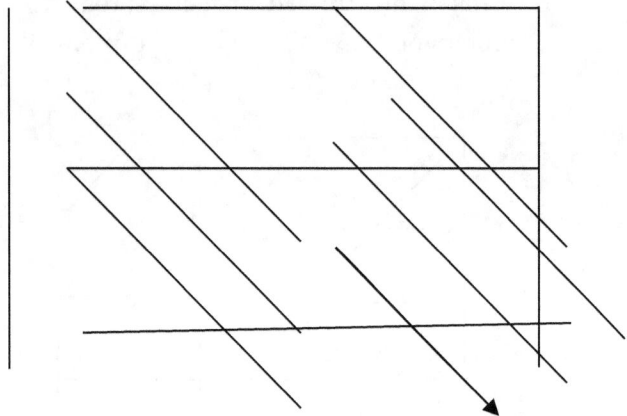

Of course, if we move that physical form rapidly enough, it transforms to something far less physically structured in a 3-D sense, and less physically dense. Here, let's just say that the sides come off of the cube as the cube transforms to something else, a new, moving, shape, a new non 3-D geometric pattern or matrix:

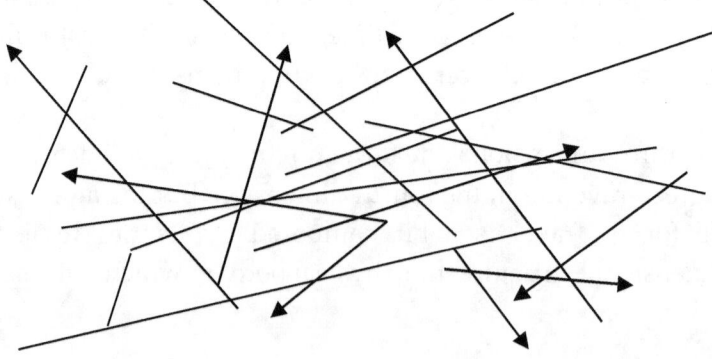

SEEING BEYOND OUR LINE OF SIGHT

The dimensions beyond your material dimension of reality may, in a sense, progress geometrically just as do the point, the line, the plane, and the three dimensional object. Yet, it is difficult for many of us to see (or sense) the progression beyond the dimension or condition of reality we think we know best, which here tends to be three dimensional (3-D) reality.

**CONSCIOUSLY MOVING THROUGH
LIFE'S CHANGES, TRANSITIONS, AND DEATHS**

24
Shed The Skin
In Moving Through

Each and every one of us reaches a point in life, usually several times, when our particular way of seeing the world, of behaving, of relating, of being -- when our particular reality -- no longer fits us. That we change over time is not surprising. Nor is that we tend to miss many of the very precious steps within our own transitions. (We see baby steps, even celebrate these, in very young children, but less so in ourselves.)

In reality, we are perpetually in transition. We are always ending and beginning, cycling, spiraling, traveling through hidden as well as visible change. The *continuum of change and transition* we live on stretches far past the conceptual limits we tend to set on it, far past our notions of biological birth and death. We can locate ourselves along the *continuum of consciousness* now and in all transition processes.

CONSCIOUSLY MOVING THROUGH
LIFE'S CHANGES, TRANSITIONS, AND DEATHS

All Deaths Are A Shedding

Nothing said herein seeks to deny the immensely profound nature of physical death. These pages simply alert us to the also very important qualities of all deaths, endings, transitions, we undergo. After all, all deaths are a shedding of what can be viewed as outgrown ways, behaviors, beliefs, lives, bodies....

We can be attuned to the approaches of these sheddings. These can indeed be viewed as *windows of opportunity*. KEY in *consciously navigating transitions* is our sensitizing ourselves to be perceptive enough to spot and sense our windows of opportunity.[47]

Not all windows are windows of opportunity. Some windows are simply openings to another part of the PATTERN TERRAIN we are moving through. Some windows are not safe windows to move through. Some windows are even sinkholes or

---

[47] For a more detailed description of these windows and other *navigation characteristics and elements*, see Book Two of NAVIGATING LIFE'S STUFF. In these NAVIGATING LIFE'S STUFF books, I define what I call the PATTERN TERRAIN we are always moving within and through. *Sensitizing ourselves* to the characteristics of our ever changing PATTERN TERRAIN assists us in ever more consciously navigating our transitions.

traps. We can sensitize ourselves to ever better detect the differences among these.[48]

Detecting Windows

We too often miss seeing that we need to shed our skins, and that we are facing opportunities to do so. (Sometimes we miss understanding which skin we need to shed, and nevertheless feel driven to shed something. This may result in the shedding of the wrong thing.)

We can even miss entirely the fact that we are already undergoing sheddings, not realizing that these are taking place, until we are either deep into their processes, completed with their processes, or well into much later sheddings.

Or, we entirely miss our sheddings, again not realizing that these have taken place, which results in our not using these well or not bringing these to completion so as to move on.

---

[48] See details regarding this important sensitization in Book Two of NAVIGATING LIFE'S STUFF.

**CONSCIOUSLY MOVING THROUGH
LIFE'S CHANGES, TRANSITIONS, AND DEATHS**

Stumbling through life and its transitions unaware is a less effective way to walk, and certainly is not *conscious navigation of transition.*

Whether we see our sheddings, shedding is as much a part of life and death as is any other function. You shed skin cells and hair every day. In cycles of every seven or so years, you recycle many of the cells in your body. Your brain sheds some cells and also continues to develop new neural connections as it ages. If you are an adult, you have, most likely, also already shed several states of mind, beliefs, and behaviors.

There may be no point in your physical life when you are not shedding or replacing or developing something. All this makes room for the new.

Most of our physical deaths take place when we have outgrown, worn out, or severely injured our physical bodies. Our bodies are then no longer the vehicles we inhabit, no longer the vehicles for the particular journey we have acquired and grown these physical bodies for.

At physical death, our physical bodies are no longer the vehicles of our evolution. Yet, our consciousness can continue to be our actual vehicle, as the consciousness can choose to live along the *continuum of consciousness*.

**CONSCIOUSLY MOVING THROUGH
LIFE'S CHANGES, TRANSITIONS, AND DEATHS**

25
How You Know Your Skin's Too Tight

This chapter considers some subtleties of change (or need for change) that we can sensitize to, in order to become more aware of the characteristics of our transition processes.

All too often the pressure to shed sneaks up on us. We finally notice that the skin of a behavior, a life, is far too tight -- that we have outgrown it the way a snake outgrows its skin.

Shedding Indications

You can harvest more from the *shedding process* by recognizing in advance when you are at its *threshold*. How do you do this? Become very alert to subtleties:

- Notice shifts in your ability to concentrate.
- Notice changes in your enthusiasm.
- Notice when you feel claustrophobic or trapped physically, emotionally, mentally.
- Notice if you are regularly exhibiting troubled behavior (which is detrimental to yourself or others).

- Notice to what degree you function on automatic -- mindlessly.
- Notice how you respond when you stop for a moment's reflection and ask yourself, "Who am I and why am I here?"
- **Notice if and when you feel your life to be taking on less meaning for you.**

If Feeling Less Meaning

If you find that your life takes on less and less meaning for you -- pay attention. There are a range of messages you, your brain, your mind, your awareness, could be sending you.

Of course, physical survival is essential. *Where physical survival itself becomes a great challenge, a range of responses to this survival pressure may appear in the mind and brain.*

If you find that your physical survival does not feel to be under pressure, look at what else may be affecting you. Again, if you find that your life is taking on less and less meaning for you, do pay attention.

What pressures are you feeling? How are these affecting you? How are you becoming aware of pressures you are

experiencing? What pressures might you be experiencing while you are not aware you are experiencing these? How might these unseen pressures be affecting you?

Be Aware

We sometimes tell ourselves what we need to know without realizing we are doing so. We may give ourselves hard to read, subtle, signs and symptoms. Or, we may send ourselves loud and clear messages.

Be aware of what you are telling yourself. Is an emotion or behavior or situation not working for you, perhaps needing an adjustment or change? Is part of, or even all of, the emotion or behavior or situation something you must amend, leave, shed?

You know when it is time to shed your skin. You may be finished with a stage or a process. Or you may be closed in, caged in, boxed in, trapped, by one or more of the patterns of your life. Perhaps you are so closed in you are losing your *self*, your own *pattern of being*, and your own *free will*. Perhaps even your sense of meaning is being affected by this.

CONSCIOUSLY MOVING THROUGH
LIFE'S CHANGES, TRANSITIONS, AND DEATHS

Getting Out

Once you allow yourself to see the truth, to detect the need for shedding, for transition out, you must let yourself out of your skin. Here's where there is, sometimes, a strong resistance. Either you or the people around you may not want you to change, or may not want you to change in a certain way.

Take steps to consciously plan and map the transition out of all or a part of a situation you need to leave or amend. Open your eyes to the windows you sense or detect are present. These are everywhere. This eye-opening, this sensitizing, is training for all in-life and seeming end-of-life transitions we will navigate.

Do not let anyone tell you that you cannot get there from here. This statement tells us not to look BEYOND OUR current LINE OF SIGHT. This statement reveals our deep programming to believe in and obey limitations we have been programmed to carry.

You, your consciousness, can go many places from here. You just need a map and a vehicle. And, your consciousness *is your vehicle*, and your consciousness *can draw its own map*.

SEEING BEYOND OUR LINE OF SIGHT

The territory you will travel is the realm of your consciousness–and the map of this territory of yours is the territory itself. This is your *continuum of consciousness*.

Why Some People Think They Prefer Physical Death

There may be times when you feel you are without the map and the vehicle. Perhaps you have not yet seen that you *already do carry within you* your map and your vehicle, your awareness, your consciousness. *Your will become increasingly aware of your great capacity to ever more consciously navigate your transitions.* For example, simply giving your awareness time to consider the material in this book opens doors and avenues in your brain, your mind, and your ever more aware consciousness.

Not seeing that you already do have the awareness involved in reading your map and driving your vehicle, you may stay quite stuck. You know the feeling: It's that no exit, trapped phase. ("Paradox" is further defined and discussed in Volume 2 of this series, ADVENTURES IN CHANGES, TRANSITIONS, AND DEATHS, and also in Volumes 8 and 9 of this series, the NAVIGATING LIFE'S STUFF books).

CONSCIOUSLY MOVING THROUGH
LIFE'S CHANGES, TRANSITIONS, AND DEATHS

Paradox is a state of self, a state of energetic confinement. Some persons remain entirely or substantially within a paradox -- the same, repeating, or similar sort of paradox -- for most of their lives. When the pressure to shed becomes unbearably great, they either develop a way out, perhaps even a *conscious transition* out, or maybe fall into a less preferable path out by becoming troubled or psychologically disturbed, or by falling sick, or perhaps dying there in the trap.

Some persons are trapped for a long, long, time. Some are not sure how to exit the trapped state, how to break free of the paradox. Some remain resistant to moving out of the emotional or behavioral or thought pattern or patterns that hold them trapped. They see no exit, no way to shed their skins.

Some accept living with the trapped sensation. They may not see, or want to see, the energy that can become available to them if they can free themselves from their traps.

Others do begin to feel, often on a deep subconscious level, that the only way out is some form of intense event, or crisis, or perhaps even physical death. And then, on some level, they may decide to get out this way. Because the decision is usually an

unconscious one, it does not seem to be a decision. Instead it is seen as an unfortunate event.

We must always pay close attention to what we are telling ourselves, to the messages and energy arrangements in our situations.

Making Physical

One of the most unfortunate developments is the moving of a troubled behavior pattern from the psychological to the physical realm. It is not surprising that many psychological and spiritual disturbances take on physical aspects (such as drug addiction, accident-prone-ness, and, of course, physical pain and illness). Beings who live in the material plane may at times pull whatever they can into a place where they can physically see it. There may be a drive to "make real" energies that are perceived but not seen.

(Note that nothing here blames persons experiencing physical pain or illness for their conditions. Also note that nothing here says that all physical pain and illness originates in the mind. Rather, this discussion considers the possibility that some emotional pain is physicalized. Indeed, scientific studies show that even emotional conditions such as depression can generate physical pain.)

The drive to *physicalize patterns* is valuable when it calls attention to energy disturbances and deeply buried, implicit, pattern addictions that might not otherwise be seen. Yet, at the same time, this physicalizing or somatization of a hidden condition can result in physical suffering without any healing or even any recognition of the condition from which it stems. Basically, you can make yourself sick pulling the energy in to physical form unless you are trained to work with it.

It is best to *detect and de-structure detrimental patterns* before they become physical or too physical. This means that one must be highly conscious of these patterns long before they make themselves visible to the physical eye. Much more may be accomplished when the work is done *beyond* the level of the physical body and physical plane, BEYOND OUR present LINE OF SIGHT. We can develop conceptual surgery on our personal behavioral, emotional, and other energy patterns, as this awareness is now possible and essential.[49]

This understanding becomes more clear as we *consciously expand* our *conscious awareness* along and throughout our *continuum of consciousness*, where we are not tied only to physicality to define and access ourselves.

Ideally, KEY transitions are conducted on the non-physical level, consciously along the continuum of consciousness itself, rather than bringing the needed transition process into physicality.

---

[49] Refer to other books in this KEYS TO CONSCIOUSNESS AND SURVIVAL SERIES such as UNVEILING THE HIDDEN INSTINCT, and also HOW TO DIE AND SURVIVE, BOOK ONE, and also Book Two of NAVIGATING LIFE'S STUFF.

**CONSCIOUSLY MOVING THROUGH
LIFE'S CHANGES, TRANSITIONS, AND DEATHS**

26
Harvest Transition

Your transitions are, in essence, *transformations of patterns.*

These patterns hold energy, and arrangements of energy. You can map these transitions, these pattern transformations. In so doing, you fine tune your *transition navigation awareness.*

You gain awareness and thus power over the course of your life and your evolution. As you grow in this understanding, you gain an increasing say in the use of your transition awareness, and of your transition energy, however this idea of transition energy registers for you.

You can sense, access, energy flowing through you and through any dimension of your reality at any moment you choose. You know this energy. You can grow to know this energy ever more, to sense its variations, fluctuations, and pattern shiftings.

**CONSCIOUSLY MOVING THROUGH
LIFE'S CHANGES, TRANSITIONS, AND DEATHS**

You have as much right to the energy flowing through you as does anyone or anything else, so long as you are not harming self or others in the use of this energy.[50]

Change May Release Energy

Do not fear healthy change. Fear of healthy change can block, congest, distort, redirect, perhaps even weaken your energy. Remember that there is, throughout the cosmos, a perpetual flow of change, in which forces are always interweaving and disentangling, contracting and expanding. Some of this motion is smooth, some of this is not. Some of this is convulsive. But all of this is change. Change is incessant.

Be Aware Of Resistance

Resisting a needed change is resisting a needed transition. This resistance risks stagnation. Being trapped a long time–or

---

[50] NOTE: You may even have more right to the energy you are producing or arranging than does anyone around you. So often, we are told otherwise as in, "your attention is needed," or "your attention is required," or "you must give of your time," or "don't be so selfish," and so on. While of course, giving of yourself makes sense in many situations, what many tend to do is forget to give of themselves to themselves, to give some of their energy to themselves as they move through their lives and transitions. Yet, our own energy and attention is valuable as we navigate our transitions, so save some of your energy for your SELF.

experiencing a long term *paradoxical energy trap*--becomes a stagnation of energy.[51]

Too many elect, of what they believe to be their own free wills, to stagnate, to go against the flow, to resist healthy change, healthy transition. This is not surprising.

We have not allowed ourselves, or have not been allowed to, fully understand the *dynamics of change and transition*.[52] We may then be held in an uninformed state, because we are more easily controlled there -- controlled by our own pattern addictions, our own political, cultural, educational, and belief systems, and likely by other forces too large and invisible for us to see.

Individual And Species Energy Flow

Because you affect your arrangement of your energy, and you release your arrangement of this energy, you are responsible

---

[51] See the definition and discussion of the *paradoxical energy trap* in NAVIGATING LIFE'S STUFF, Book One and then Book Two.
[52] Note that the subtitle of the NAVIGATING LIFE'S STUFF books is: DYNAMICS OF PERSONAL CHANGE. Refer to these books for further discussion of these dynamics.

for what your energy does and where it goes during the time your energy flows through and from you.

This means that, you, as a responsible being, must learn to master the flow of your energy in and out of life transitions and dimensions of reality. You must be as conscious as possible of the phases of transition and the transcendence of phases.[53] You must be ever alert for indication of the need for shedding, and of windows through which you, we, can move our awareness.

You can remain ever more conscious through ever more of your transitions -- physical and non-physical. You can further advance your awareness in transitions in order to be certain you do not inadvertently – without meaning to -- surrender, sign over, or land your energy in a place where you lose say in, lose free will in, its right use.

It is your responsibility, then, to prepare for the appropriate and conscious harvest of your energy which takes

---

[53] See *Volume 8* in this series, titled *NAVIGATING LIFE'S STUFF, BOOK ONE*, where phases and patterns are defined and mapped, where the basic underlying pattern phases are shown to include these key patterns: STRUGGLE, PARADOX, INSIGHT, and ELEVATION. See also Volume 2 in this KEYS TO CONSCIOUSNESS AND SURVIVAL SERIES, titled ADVENTURES IN CHANGES, TRANSITIONS, AND DEATHS.

place during and following each and every one of your in-life and seeming end-of-life transitions. When we, as individuals, increasingly accept this responsibility, we increase the ability of our entire species to do the same....

Prepare For The Harvest

To best prepare for your harvest of your energy, take conscious control of your life's processes, transitions. Although you cannot control all the events within and around you, you can direct, navigate, your journey through these.

- Become sensitive to the phases, sheddings, and windows that appear during transitions.

- Notice the energy that is available to you as you harvest your energy during your transitions. You can use this energy to move through your transitions to new arrangements of your energy, new arrangements of your *self*.

- You may want to give yourself physical images, ideas, for tracking transition processes.

**CONSCIOUSLY MOVING THROUGH
LIFE'S CHANGES, TRANSITIONS, AND DEATHS**

- For example, during any difficult transition, you may choose to stay focused on a high point within what you feel is your physical body, or a metaphor for a physical body. It is best to select either the area in what you imagine to be the center of the forehead or the top of the head to stay connected to.

- Hold on to this connection, keep returning to the idea of it, as if there were a cord attached to it.

- If you want to let go of this cord you may, but only do so quite consciously, as if you are knowingly releasing the reigns while riding a wild horse.

- Check the *transition terrain* out beforehand: Are there any traps or trick windows leading to dead ends or undesirable nested loops -- seeming no-escape repeat pathways -- for your energy?

- Ask yourself: Can you see clearly what is calling you and coming at you? (Other books in this series will detail the various cord releases that you might undertake at this juncture. For now, letting go, yet being conscious as you do, is enough of a description.)

SEEING BEYOND OUR LINE OF SIGHT

- Should you elect this form of release, do so knowing that you are freeing your energy for absorption by your environment in time, in space, in the cosmos. The harvest of your life force will no longer be specifically yours then.

- To turn over your harvest, the release of energy brought about by your transition process, is not a detrimental choice, so long as you know well where you are sending it. No matter how challenging the turning-over phase, this release can be most exalting.

- **However, stay conscious during transition processes to be aware of the option to elect *not to surrender your energy*.**

- No matter how rough your ride, how tortured your transition process, it is your option to keep your eyes -- *your conceptual and intuitive interdimensional sensory mechanisms* – open, and notice what presences or fields (forces, factors, systems) are there to receive or even absorb or even highjack your energy.

- Whether you are dying a death of a behavior or dying a physical death, you can take responsibility for the energy you release when old patterns die.

- The harvest is yours. Stay conscious of this.

- However, do not sell your product, the arrangement of energy you have cultivated, your consciousness itself, at the market, unless the exchange is toward an ever more right use and freedom of will. If you feel unprepared to make such an assessment, keep your energy under your wing and continue to evolve it and your awareness of it, your aware consciousness.

- Even if you do feel prepared, remember that it can remain your own choice whether to turn over your energy, whether to surrender your personal consciousness to another presence or field—OR TO HOLD ON TO YOUR PERSONAL CONSCIOUSNESS.

- You can continue to evolve your SELF as an awareness, as a matrix of SELF, as your *personal aware consciousness*.

- **You can choose to survive.**

27
Cosmic Democracy

Although, as beings living in the physical plane, we are programmed not to see the full implications of this reality, we do live in a multi-dimensional reality at all times. There is a *cosmic democracy* practiced here. We can tap into this, access this arena, once we know this exists.

Each and every one of us has the free and equal right to participate consciously in the processes of **conscious evolution** and **conscious_ness_ evolution**. Each and every one of us can participate in the transmission of our awareness, our aware consciousness, as we traverse and expand along both the *communal and the personal continuums of consciousness*.

Once we access the awareness that is our birthright, then we can accept the shift of ourselves from being seen as primarily, and in some cases only, physical dimension beings, to the *continuum of consciousness* where we already do live.

Here, surviving takes on new dimensions, as do the notions of living and dying processes, which are all about constant ongoing transitions -- rather than an absolute ending to life.

SEEING BEYOND OUR LINE OF SIGHT

PART SIX

REVOLUTION

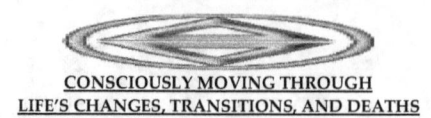

SEEING BEYOND OUR LINE OF SIGHT

28
Ride Personal Expansion
Into Personal And Species Power

As a Human living in a 3-D physical plane biological Human body, you know something of the ordeals faced by life forms living in the third and fourth dimensions, the physical plane and the time it moves through. When understood, these physical plane ordeals can encourage awareness and expansion along the inter-dimensional *continuum of consciousness*. When misunderstood, these can distract from such awareness and its expansion, and from survival potential.

The journey through your Human incarnation can be superbly remarkable and yet superbly challenging. The potential for what is called "the quickening of the soul" is profoundly immense during your Human incarnation.

Try to remember this in positive as well as difficult living moments. And try to receive this message in its entirety at the hour of your physical death.

Denial Of More

As a physicalized Human being living on the physical plane planet Earth, it may be easy for you to think that there exists nothing but this third dimension -- that there is only material reality and nothing else -- and, therefore, that all life forms and celestial forms have physical bodies.

Although a Human being living in the 3-D physical plane often begins to feel there might be more to her or his reality than meets the physical eye, the assumption that nothing living can really exist without a three dimensional body (and its brain) can persist.

As the *continuum of consciousness awareness* of Human beings further advances, personal evolving of additional higher, less physical, domains of the self can take place. As a life form extends its awareness of, *even occupation of, reality to beyond the base of the physical realm,* that being becomes more mobile, more *inter-dimensionally mobile*. Try to encourage this trend in yourself. You will be contributing to your own and your species' evolution.

The full essence of the universe is one which likely lies beyond the grasp of the existing Human intellect. Fortunately, the collective Human mind is beginning to progress through the development of its intellect into a new form of intelligence where it may someday (again) be an active cosmic intelligence.

Consciousness Technology

Consciously further awaken your consciousnesses. To do so, become ever more adept in your own personal *consciousness technology*. This is the technology by which your consciousness can become highly aware of itself and profoundly enhance its functioning and freedom along the *continuum of consciousness*.

You can evolve increasing degrees of consciousness. You are already part of a *life system* of conscious interaction -- an energetic *awareness system* which has its own form of government and even economy.

But how much freedom is available to you within the system you "belong to"? An ever higher level of *aware* **consciousness can be achieved to: transcend the lower level physical plane systems and patterns in which we (believe we)**

presently live; and, to preserve our free will across the dimensions.

This is KEY in consciously navigating transitions, in *consciously surviving transitions as a personal consciousness.*

Believing In More And Finding It

Turn on the light! Death is not what you may believe it to be! Nothing dies in the so-called "conventional" sense, because nothing stops moving -- matter is always in motion, whether organic or inorganic.

Examine information for truth. Humans must do this. Truth has been severely distorted by language and culture (and other less visible forces). The precious consciousness of Humanity is buried within an elaborate hierarchy of distortion that veils truth.

Unfolding Our Awareness

We have a right to the awareness we carry within us, awaiting us. We can become who we truly are, a species of consciousness.

SEEING BEYOND OUR LINE OF SIGHT

Let this unfolding begin within you. When you are ready to be ever more aware of what is and is not actual unfiltered truth, you will recognize this as it comes to you. This is your truth regarding who you are and where you live, where you locate yourself along your *continuum of awareness and consciousness.*

You can share, with the collective awareness pool, the awareness generated by your transformation of your own aware consciousness. You can contribute to a global, and a cosmic, transformation that will help end what may be the cultivation, wasting, and kidnapping of your, our, physical plane energies.

The movement of the location of the SELF, of the personal awareness, of the personal consciousness, from only or primarily the physical plane to…

THE CONTINUUM OF CONSCIOUSNESS
is both a minor and a revolutionary shift.

Free Will Must Survive

Death itself is a transition of energy. Where we can bring our awareness to the death process, *death can be a transition of awareness itself. This is where death can be an expansion along the continuum of existence.*

Once we understand this, an additional elaboration on the notion of death is necessary: There is a great difference between transitional and absolute death. This difference relates to the presence of our free will.

When free will disappears, this will be the absolute death of free will. Matter and energy may live on eternally, however, our free will may be permanently eliminated.

This end of free will would not be an adventure in change, transition, or death. This would be the end of the life of an energy force you have come to call "freedom." Do not allow this transition into an entirely mechanical, programmed, robotic, will-less, soul-less universe to happen. Stay consciously aware, as aware and as conscious as possible, through all in-life and seeming end of life and even also after-life transitions.

Wherever free will is diminished yet still present, fuel its return to its fullest potential. Draw upon the life force to fuel free will.

SEEING BEYOND OUR LINE OF SIGHT

free will

is fueled by the

LIFE FORCE

**CONSCIOUSLY MOVING THROUGH
LIFE'S CHANGES, TRANSITIONS, AND DEATHS**

29
Embrace The Revolution Brought By Conscious Death

They say we think, therefore we are. But who are we?

And, is this action or process we call "thinking" restricted to the biological brain? If so, how can we know this for certain?

What thinks? The brain? The mind? The awareness? The consciousness? Is there a difference? Can we detect the difference?

How would we know whether non-physical life forms think when all we have here are measures of the physical plane thinking processes of the biological brain?

Basically, via our present tools, we can neither prove nor disprove the existence of non-biological non-physical thought, or of non-biological non-physical consciousness-es.

See The Option

No matter what opinion or belief system we bring to the table, and no matter what is presently the case, we may have the option of developing capacities we may or may not presently have or detect ourselves already having.

We have a consciousness, we already do know this.

That we can survive as an awareness, an aware consciousness, may be an option we have, should we choose to evolve or develop this option. Basically, we can choose to SEE and extend and exist BEYOND OUR present LINE OF SIGHT.

Our Human Mind-Brain

Seemingly contained in a skull no larger than a deflated soccer ball and physically manifested in the form of a wrinkled blob we call brain, the Human mind-brain is a cagey, intractable entity -- difficult to locate but boundaryless, capable of amazing feats but weak and fallible, seemingly autonomous and yet tending toward the convenience of supposedly survival-oriented preprogramming which often results in undesirable, sometimes terrible, habitual behaviors and other pattern addictions.

One of the toughest of all our brain's pattern addictions is our addiction to our physical plane reality as being our only reality. Somehow, we allow our dependence on, our deep reliance on, our seeming reality, to be a reality check on all reality. We cling to what we think **IS**, refusing to let it die unless we are pushed to the edge and lose control or fitfully relinquish it. And then there is a tortured transition or death, rather than a fruitful one.

- When the world as we know it, the reality upon which we have become so dependent, dies, do we die too? Must we die too?

- They say that we live; therefore we die. But who says this? Who lives? What dies?

- **Could we be prisoner of a lie? Whose lie could this be?**

Politics Of Death

Could death be something different from what we have come to believe it is? Can we break free of the shackles of our realities and see through our fears, our sufferings, our difficult transitions, our mental, emotional, spiritual, and even physical deaths?

Can we look through the veil of deception that humanity has been evolved, or even programmed to, live beneath, and see the truth about ourselves, about the *lifeform of consciousness* we actually are? Yes. But first we must be willing, be daring enough, to ask:

Are we programmed to die physical death? Why do each and every one of our biological cells have a genetic plan to die off after a certain number of divisions?

Are we genetically programmed to die physical deaths? Or are we genetically programmed to believe that we have to die and that physical death is final and is the end of us? And is this programmed-in belief so all powerful that it controls us, kills us, threatens to make our deaths final?

SEEING BEYOND OUR LINE OF SIGHT

Have we been brainwashed into acceptance of a lie about dying. What for? What force or intelligence or energy could have focused upon our genetic coding so closely as to create such a limited reality in our minds?[54]

We must dare to ask: Are we biological, fleshy robots? Do we reflect a sallow mechanical light in our eyes, the light of will-less-ness, the glow of hypnotization? Have we succumbed to a daze in modern times or have we always been part of a programmed-in mindlessness? Are we biotech at its finest? Or biotech gone wrong?

If Earth is a fantastic macrocosmic laboratory, are we prisoner-subjects in a massive experiment too large for our Human minds to fathom? Could our seeing what is going on lead to startling discoveries regarding our captors?

Perhaps we can capture control of our wills and set them free. Only a revolution of Human awareness can free us. But

---

[54] See detailed discussion of this factor or force affecting our minds and brains in the OVERRIDING THE EXTINCTION SCENARIO books, Volumes 5 and 6 in this KEYS TO CONSCIOUSNESS AND SURVIVAL SERIES.

what would this freedom look like? Would it be much different from way we live and look now?

Can we really be free as long as we are subject to the enslavement of inherited and acquired, genetic and neurological, programming tying our perceptions to only our biological realities – and blocking our fully aware access to our *continuum of consciousness* where we can truly be, exist, survive?[55]

---

[55] See detailed explanation of this limiting and blocking of our access in the OVERRIDING THE EXTINCTION SCENARIO books.

30
The Right To Know
The Art And Science Of
Conscious Dying And Surviving

While end-of-life death, physical death, can be said to be a great teacher and releaser, this is <u>not</u> the route to resolve situations where what is needed is the shedding of a behavioral, or emotional, or even belief or thought, pattern.

Too often, some people find themselves unconsciously stumbling into terminal disease or impulsive or irresponsible suicide. This *in no way blames* people for moving into these pathways.

What we want to do here is to understand that there may be routes for the consciousness to sense and navigate needs for shedding that can take place before a physical death exit is determined.[56]

---

[56] For further discussion of the notion of *shedding*, see the NAVIGATING LIFE'S STUFF books, Volumes 8 and 9 in this KEYS TO CONSCIOUSNESS AND SURVIVAL SERIES.

**CONSCIOUSLY MOVING THROUGH
LIFE'S CHANGES, TRANSITIONS, AND DEATHS**

We also must advance the **art and science of conscious dying**. This has to begin with the art and science of **conscious transitioning**, both **in-life and seeming end-of-life transitioning**.

NOTE: This is also not an argument against conscious physical death as a respectable way out of the skin of a life that one has outgrown. However, the *art and science of intentionally dying* must be very carefully taught and learned with a preparation and care few cultures have thus far developed.

We already know much more about *self-deliverance* than we realize. Yet, preparing to make such a decision may take a lifetime of preparation. Certainly, there are persons who give advice regarding medicinal and mechanical means of dying. This book does not address, or offer opinion on, these forms of euthanasia, etc.

However, there are many ways of detaching from the body that require no chemical or medical assistance, no outside intervention. These must be better understood and researched. It is time for this knowledge to become readily available. (Some of these techniques are discussed in depth in Volumes 4, 11, and 14 in this KEYS TO CONSCIOUSNESS AND SURVIVAL SERIES, which are the HOW TO DIE AND SURVIVE books.)

31
Sense The Momentum

If you have ever been driving a fast moving vehicle and then had to abruptly stop, you have experienced the *forward motion of the body and its energy*. The body continues to move forward in space and time even after the vehicle has stopped. Similarly, in a more expanded and infinite way, physical death offers a parallel – offers a far more powerful, perhaps even infinite, *extension of momentum*. The personal physical body may stop, however the personal consciousness may move on in an extension of momentum as…

THE LIFE FORCE DOES NOT DIE.

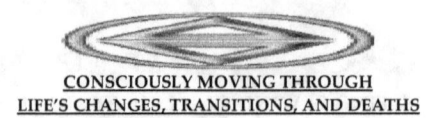
**CONSCIOUSLY MOVING THROUGH
LIFE'S CHANGES, TRANSITIONS, AND DEATHS**

SEEING BEYOND OUR LINE OF SIGHT

Epilog

Thank you for joining in understanding in a deep way that transitions are continuous, that your personal consciousness has the option of being continuous—and that you can know this for your *self*, for those around you, for Humanity, for all life on this planet we call Earth and BEYOND.

This journey is yours. So make it your own! Master the ride of your life. This is what the journey of life is about – seeing its process as always in transition, and seeing the survival options.

The suppression of knowledge that is KEY to the survival of your awareness as an aware consciousness, to the survival of all of us, must end. The time has indeed come for us to know what we have a right to know, for the removal of our ignorance.

We can unlock the doors to our *continuum of consciousness*. This is our space, territory we can rightfully occupy. We have a right to SEE BEYOND OUR LINE OF SIGHT.

We can dare to survive.

**CONSCIOUSLY MOVING THROUGH
LIFE'S CHANGES, TRANSITIONS, AND DEATHS**

SEEING BEYOND OUR LINE OF SIGHT

Never Ending Stream

By what amazing grace
have we arrived here,
lost and found
ending and beginning
again.
The thread, the spirit, of life
weaves on and on
as we intertwine
with all around
and all within
and all eternity.
A never ending stream of
all things we were,
we are, and
we will be . . . .

**CONSCIOUSLY MOVING THROUGH
LIFE'S CHANGES, TRANSITIONS, AND DEATHS**

APPENDICES

**CONSCIOUSLY MOVING THROUGH
LIFE'S CHANGES, TRANSITIONS, AND DEATHS**

SEEING BEYOND OUR LINE OF SIGHT

BOOKLIST AND RECOMMENDED BOOKS, EBOOKS, AUDIOBOOKS, PROGRAMS

KEYS TO CONSCIOUSNESS AND SURVIVAL SERIES
by Dr. Angela Brownemiller

Volume 14
How To Die and Survive: Book Three
Key Insights, Messages, And Collected How To Die And Survive Concepts, Processes, and Exercises For Living, Dying and Surviving Here and Beyond

Volume 11
How To Die and Survive: Book Two
*Extending Our Interdimensional Awareness:
Next Concepts For Living and Dying*
****

Volume 10
Seeing Beyond Our Line of Sight
*Consciously Moving Through Life's
Changes, Transitions, and Deaths*
****

Volume 9
**Navigating Life's Stuff–
Dynamics of Personal Change, Book Two**
*Keys to Consciously Moving Through
Our Processes and Their Patterns*
****

Volume 8
**Navigating Life's Stuff –
Dynamics of Personal Change, Book One**
*Sensitizing to and Navigating
Our Patterns and Their Processes*

**CONSCIOUSLY MOVING THROUGH
LIFE'S CHANGES, TRANSITIONS, AND DEATHS**

****

Volume 7
Keys To Accessing The Beyond
*Expansion, Elevation,
Transmigration,
Survival
Practices And Concepts*
****

Volume 6
Overriding the Extinction Scenario, Part <u>Two</u>
*<u>Raising</u> The Bar On The
Evolution Of The Human Species*
****

Volume 5
Overriding the Extinction Scenario, Part <u>One</u>
*<u>Detecting</u> The Bar On The
Evolution Of The Human Species*
****

Volume 4
How to Die and Survive
*Interdimensional Psychology,
Consciousness, And Survival:
Concepts For Living And Dying*
****

Volume 3
Unveiling the Hidden Instinct
*Understanding Our
Interdimensional Survival Awareness*
****

Volume 2
Adventures In Changes, Transitions, And Deaths
****

Volume 1
Keys to Self
****

SEEING BEYOND OUR LINE OF SIGHT

BOOKLIST AND RECOMMENDED READING
Continued....

Metaterra Chronicles Collection
Angela Brownemiller

Ask Dr. Angela Series
Angela Brownemiller

The Bloodwin Code (Episode Books 1, 2, 3, 4, 5)
Angela Brownemiller

Transcending Addiction
Angela Brownemiller

Gestalting Addiction
Angela Brownemiller

Contact us for information on the special
Science Fiction Series
on these consciousness and survival topics.
Email:
DrAngelaBrownemiller@gmail.com

Note:
These books should be listed on Amazon.com and numerous other book distributor websites. If not finding these books on these sites and or in book stores, request these bookstores order these books, and or contact Amazon.com or Metaterra® Publications at Metaterra.com and/or **www.DrAngela.com** or the author, Dr. Angela Brownemiller as DrAngelaBrownemiller@gmail.com. In bookstores, on the Internet, and on Amazon, check for both Angela BrowneEmiller and also under last name, Browne-Miller. Thank you.

**CONSCIOUSLY MOVING THROUGH
LIFE'S CHANGES, TRANSITIONS, AND DEATHS**

SEEING BEYOND OUR LINE OF SIGHT

For more information on author
Angela Brownemiller's
mind-body-spirit-consciousness
concepts and processes
and her other work, see:
DrAngela.com

The works of **Angela Brownemiller**
are brought to you by:

METATERRA® PUBLICATIONS
(**and numerous other publishers**, see Amazon.com).
For copies of print books, audiobooks, and ebooks
by this author,
see Amazon.com
or contact us at
DrAngela.com

To take part in our events and workshops,
and or
for personal consultations
in person or by telephone or online,
contact us at
DrAngelaBrownemiller@gmail.com

CONSCIOUSLY MOVING THROUGH
LIFE'S CHANGES, TRANSITIONS, AND DEATHS

GET THE TRUTH ABOUT ADDICTION
Life-changing insights into the reality of
patterns, habits, addictions, and obsessions
in our lives and minds.

Now in powerfully narrated AUDIOBOOK
as well as PAPERBACK and EBOOK forms!

**SEEING THE
HIDDEN FACE
OF
ADDICTION**

Detecting and Confronting This Invasive Presence
Dr. Angela Brownemiller

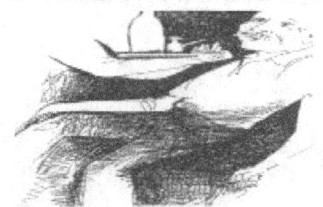

SEEING THE HIDDEN FACE OF ADDICTION
can be found on Amazon.com and DrAngela.com

SEEING BEYOND OUR LINE OF SIGHT

VOLUMES 8 & 9 in the
KEYS TO CONSCIOUSNESS AND SURVIVAL SERIES

Can we better understand the journeys we travel through in our lives? Can we detect and work with the patterns and processes we are forming, living within, and moving through? How much can we see about the patterns we form, and sometimes feel we cannot change, are caught in? How do we sensitize ourselves to the patterning processes we are engaged in? Find your way through the maze of life. See:

NAVIGATING LIFE'S STUFF:
DYNAMICS OF PERSONAL CHANGE, BOOK ONE
Sensitizing to and Navigating Our Patterns and Their Processes

NAVIGATING LIFE'S STUFF:
DYNAMICS OF PERSONAL CHANGE, BOOK TWO
Keys to Consciously Moving Through Our Passages and Their Patterns

Now in Paperback, Audiobook, and Ebook forms.
Find these and other books by Angela Brownemiller on
Amazon.com and Audible.com and DrAngela.com

CONSCIOUSLY MOVING THROUGH
LIFE'S CHANGES, TRANSITIONS, AND DEATHS

Volumes 5 and 6 in the
KEYS TO CONSCIOUSNESS AND SURVIVAL SERIES
By DR. ANGELA BROWNEMILLER:

OVERRIDING THE EXTINCTION SCENARIO, PART ONE:
DETECTING THE BAR ON THE
EVOLUTION OF THE HUMAN SPECIES

and reach more deeply into all this with…
OVERRIDING THE EXTINCTION SCENARIO, PART TWO:
RAISING THE BAR ON THE
EVOLUTION OF THE HUMAN SPECIES

Now in Paperback, Audiobook, and Ebook forms.
Find these and other books by Angela Brownemiller
on Amazon.com and DrAngela.com

SEEING BEYOND OUR LINE OF SIGHT

Volume 3 in this
KEYS TO CONSCIOUSNESS AND SURVIVAL SERIES:
UNVEILING THE HIDDEN INSTINCT
by Dr. Angela Brownemiller

Every day, we are presented with minor and major opportunities, reasons, even needs, to understand the nature of transitioning, shifting, from one state of mind, one way of being, one way of seeing the world, from one reality to another. In this sense, we are frequently calling upon ourselves to shift ourselves and our consciousness-es from one dimension of ourselves to another. At times, we may even sense that our well-being, perhaps even our survival, depends upon such a shift. ... Should we at some point find the survival level need to shift ourselves across ways of seeing the world, realities, dimensions, even perhaps from physical to non-physical and back, it is essential we have at least already considered the concepts involved. This book introduces, via metaphor, minor and major shift awareness-es, making these understandings accessible to us should we need these for everyday challenges as well as potentially profound survival reasons.

**CONSCIOUSLY MOVING THROUGH
LIFE'S CHANGES, TRANSITIONS, AND DEATHS**

Volume 10 in this
KEYS TO CONSCIOUSNESS AND SURVIVAL SERIES:
SEEING BEYOND OUR LINE OF SIGHT
by Dr. Angela Brownemiller

SEEING BEYOND OUR LINE OF SIGHT: CONSCIOUSLY MOVING THROUGH LIFE'S CHANGES, TRANSITIONS, AND DEATHS ... is a simple yet profound book offering subtle yet major shifts in the way we think about changes, transitions, endings, and deaths. Here, we can see that we have the capability of holding and empowering our conscious selves as we move through events, changes, transitions, even emotional, even physical, death processes. ... The journey this book takes us on opens doors to finding our way through challenging, trying, even very difficult, events and passages in our lives. ... That we can survive is central as we undergo all minor and major transitions in our lives. ... Find yourself, know yourself, guide yourself through the minor and major transition and death processes you face during your life. You can define who and what you are for yourself. You can open this option in your mind, the option that you can develop this knowledge of yourself, and then carry this knowledge of yourself through this life, and perhaps also on beyond this lifetime.

SEEING BEYOND OUR LINE OF SIGHT

DETECTING THE OMEGA DECEPTION

NOTES FROM THE FRONT

ANGELA BROWNEMILLER
Metaterra© Publications

THE TRUE STORY OF THIS AUTHOR'S DISCOVERY OF THE OMEGA DECEPTION.

Find this and other books by Angela Brownemiller on
Amazon.com and at **DrAngela.com**
DrAngelaBrownemiller@gmail.com

**CONSCIOUSLY MOVING THROUGH
LIFE'S CHANGES, TRANSITIONS, AND DEATHS**

Ancient teachings, messagings through time and space,
Earth herself, are calling us now.

SEEING BEYOND OUR LINE OF SIGHT

AUTHOR CONTACT
For Consults, Workshops, Events, Appearances:
www.DrAngela.com

for
Paperback, Audiobook, and Ebook
versions of this and other books
by this author
Dr. Angela Brownemiller

DrAngelaBrownemiller@gmail.com

see
www.Amazon.com
and
www.DrAngela.com

CONSCIOUSLY MOVING THROUGH
LIFE'S CHANGES, TRANSITIONS, AND DEATHS

ABOUT THE AUTHOR
Dr. Angela Brownemiller
Dr. Angela®

Dr. Angela Brownemiller, also known as Dr. Angela®, is an author, journalist, social thinker, clinician, psychotherapist, trainer, speaker, and creator of the ASK DR. ANGELA Series of broadcasts, podcasts, books, audiobooks, Ebooks, and programs. The views of Angela Brownemiller are centered on the great potential of the Human mind, heart, and soul, and on the rights of all of us, who and whatever we are (or think we are). Dr. Angela Brownemiller views the Human consciousness as a wealth of opportunity for exploration, insight, knowledge—and survival.

DrAngelaBrownemiller@gmail.com
DrAngela.com

SEEING BEYOND OUR LINE OF SIGHT

www.ingramcontent.com/pod-product-compliance
Lightning Source LLC
Chambersburg PA
CBHW071957220426
43662CB00009B/1173